DARTHUR

NOTES

including
  • *Introduction*
  • *Life of Malory*
  • *Malory and the Legend of Arthur*
  • *The Characters*
  • *Summaries and Commentaries*
  • *Review Questions*
  • *Selected Bibliography*

by
John Gardner, Ph.D.
Department of English
Southern Illinois University

INCORPORATED
LINCOLN, NEBRASKA 68501

Editor

Gary Carey, M.A.
University of Colorado

Consulting Editor

James L. Roberts, Ph.D.
Department of English
University of Nebraska

ISBN 0-8220-0726-6
© Copyright 1970
by
Cliffs Notes, Inc.
All Rights Reserved
Printed in U.S.A.

2000 Printing

Cliffs Notes, Inc.   Lincoln, Nebraska

CONTENTS

Le Morte Darthur

INTRODUCTION

Le Morte Darthur, completed in 1469 or 1470 and printed by Caxton in abridged form in 1485, is the first major work of prose fiction in English and remains today one of the greatest. It is the carefully constructed myth of the rise and fall of a powerful kingdom — a legendary kingdom, but perhaps also, obliquely, the real English kingdom which in Malory's day seemed as surely doomed by its own corruption as the ancient realm of King Arthur. Malory's myth explores the forces which bring kingdoms into being and the forces, internal and external, which destroy them. The power of the myth goes beyond whatever political implications it had in its day — set up in, for instance, the parallels Malory introduced between Arthur's reign and the reign of Henry V (discussed below). Malory's grim vision has relevance for any kingdom or civilization: the very forces which make civilization necessary must in the end, if Malory is right, bring it to ruin.

What holds the myth together is not only its undeviating philosophy of doom. In *Le Morte Darthur* Malory created, or gave new personality to, some of the most striking characters to be found in all English literature: King Arthur himself, the tragic hero; Launcelot, the noblest knight in the world, torn by a conflict of loyalties which must result in his destruction of all he loves best; Sir Gawain, vengeful and treacherous but steadfast in loyalty to his king; Queen Guinevere, emblem of courtly courtesy, generous but also fierce in jealousy; and many more. Another force binding the legend together is Malory's fascination with deadly paradox — events which simultaneously support and undermine the kingdom. For instance, the murder of all children born on May Day, which Merlin arranges to help Arthur escape his predestined death at Mordred's hands, fails to kill Mordred but turns many powerful lords against Arthur — above all, King Lot and a part of his house, doomed themselves but established from the outset as the focus and central cause of Arthur's doom. The legend is also held together by atmosphere. Arthur's realm draws together the ancient days of Celtic magic and irrationality, the by-gone age of Christian miracles, and the fifteenth-century England Malory's readers knew—an England which, Malory suggests, is not as rational or divinely protected as it foolishly imagines.

Not that Malory's vision is wholly black. His legend has moments of great tenderness as well as comedy, and his characters' values are real and noble values; but they are values which mutually conflict and must in the end prove destructive. When the world collapses under Malory's heroes, they are robbed even of the "existential" satisfaction of such characters as Gide's Theseus, who says at the end of it all, "I have lived!" For Malory there is knowledge, but no satisfaction. Except in the case of saints like Galahad, there is only the pattern of human ambition, remorse, penance, and sorrowful death. The ancient British idea of the protector-king comes down, in Malory, to Arthur's words to Sir Bedivere as the king is rowed, mortally wounded, to Avalon:

> Then sir Bedwere cryed and seyd,
> "A, my lorde Arthur, what shall becom of me, now ye go frome me and leve me here alone amonge myne enemyes?"
> "Comforte thyselff," seyde the kynge, "and do as well as thou mayste, for in me ys no truste for to truste in."

THE TEXT

The standard edition of Malory's *Morte Darthur* is *The Works of Sir Thomas Malory*, ed., Eugène Vinaver in three volumes (Oxford, Clarendon Press, 1947; reprinted with corrections 1948). This is not Caxton's famous text but another (much closer to Malory's original) which was discovered in 1934. The spelling of names in this text, as in Caxton's, is inconsistent; and in some cases it is doubtful that the scribe used the right name at all. It may be that the manuscript which reached the scribe was confused, incomplete, or in bad repair, and he simply did what he could with it, or it may be that Malory himself allowed inconsistencies to creep in.

This volume of Notes is based on Vinaver's edition. The spelling of names used here is based, generally, on the more common spellings in Vinaver, but sometimes on what has become standard critical practice. As for the title of Malory's book, the Notes follow the practice which has become normal in recent criticism rather than the earlier standard, *Morte d'Arthur,* or Vinaver's very general title (based on his belief that the tales were not unified), *The Works of Sir Thomas Malory.* Titles used here for the eight main sections and for divisions within some of these sections are adapted from Vinaver but are shortened and simplified. For instance, Vinaver's title for Section VI, "The Tale of the Sankgreal Briefly Drawn Out of French, Which Is a Tale Chronicled for One of the Truest and One of the Holiest That Is in This World" is reduced in these Notes to "The Holy Grail."

THE LIFE OF MALORY

At the end of *Le Morte Darthur,* Malory wrote, "...I pray you all praye for my soule; for this book was ended the ix yere of the reygne of kyng edward the fourth by syr Thomas Maleore knyght...." Details elsewhere in his book reveal that he was a prisoner at the time of his writing. On this basis the author of *Le Morte Darthur* is traditionally identified as Sir Thomas Malory of Newbold Revell, who was repeatedly imprisoned between 1451 and 1460, and possibly later. This identification has never been certain and has recently been thrown into serious doubt: the writer may have been another Thomas Malory. Nevertheless, the traditional identification is still widely accepted and has played so important a part in literary folklore that it is worth preserving, if only as a curiosity.

The outlaw Malory was from an old Warwickshire family uneasily aligned with the House of York until the mid-1460's, when Warwick shifted to the Lancastrian camp. Malory was in his twenties when he succeeded to the ancestral estate. He served with the Earl of Warwick at Calais in 1436, was married a few years later, and in 1449 acquired a second estate, that of his sister's husband. All this time he was, as far as we know, a respectable and perhaps well-off citizen. In 1450 he turned out-law—and with a vengeance. Between 1450 and 1451 he was charged with several major crimes—robbery, two cattle raids, several extortions, a rape, and an attempted murder. He was jailed but escaped by swimming a moat and immediately after his escape sank to what was for medieval men the darkest of depravities—robbing churches. He broke into the Abbey of the Blessed Mary of Coombe, opened two of the abbot's chests, and stole various sacred objects and two bags of money. He came back the next night with accomplices, broke eighteen doors, in-sulted the abbot, and stole more money. He was again arrested and remained in prison for three years (1451-1454), except for a short time outside in 1452. When he was released he returned to his criminal activities, was again jailed, again broke out. He was granted a royal pardon in 1455, probably by the Duke of York, and managed to serve for his shire in Parliament for a year; but two years later he was in debtors' prison (Ludgate); and he went to Newgate Prison later (1459). He may have been in prison in 1468, when Edward IV extended his pardon to the Lancastrians but excluded "Thomas Malorie, miles." He may have been re-leased upon the restoration of Henry VI in October, 1470. He died March 14, 1471, and was buried in the chapel of St. Francis at the Grey Friars near Newgate in the suburbs of London.

Although Thomas Malory the highwayman-knight may not in fact have been the author of *Le Morte Darthur*, his criminal activities are no evidence either for or against his claim to au-thorship of the work. The author of *Le Morte Darthur* says at the end of his book that he is "the seruaunt of Ihesu both day and nyght," and throughout the book the stiff code of chivalry is played against humane and flexible Christian charity. On the other hand, Malory's myth of Arthur is essentially secular in its focus. Even the Grail Quest, as Malory treats it, is more secular than holy and ironic in spirit: it shows nobility of soul and, at the same time, through its slaughter of many of Arthur's knights, it dangerously weakens the kingdom. If the God of Malory's universe is as much a God of love as a ruler of destiny, Merlin—part man, part wizard, part devil—is his only available prophet. What the author of *Le Morte Darthur* knows best is battle, jeal-ousy, sexual lust, sudden rage, frustrated idealism, and the waste of human potential.

MALORY AND THE LEGEND OF ARTHUR

The earliest recorded tradition concerning Arthur represents him as a leader of the Britons against the Anglo-Saxon invaders. He is supposed to have won the battle of Badon Hill in the sixth century. The battle itself is historical, and since the name Arthur derives from the common Roman name *Artorius,* it seems likely that the Arthur legend may have begun in the heroism of a real man, one of the Romans who shared the plight of the Celts when the Anglo-Saxons struck. The British historian Gildas, who finished his *De Excidio et Conquestu Britanniae* around 540, tells of the battle but says nothing of Arthur. The hero himself first appears in a ninth-century history, the *Historia Brittonum,* allegedly drawn from earlier histories. The *Historia Brittonum,* begun by a man called Nennius and expanded by later writers, reports that Arthur, though not a British king himself, commanded the British forces and won twelve great victories, one of them the battle of Badon Hill, where Arthur alone killed 960 men. Later in this history the writers speak of a stone bearing the footprint of Arthur's dog, Cabal, and of the tomb of Arthur's son. A still later history, the *Annales Cambriae,* is the first to tell of Arthur's final battle, in 537, against "Medraut" — Mordred.

Though histories give little space to Arthur until the twelfth century, he was apparently a firmly established folk hero. He is the central figure in numerous ancient Welsh and Irish legends (impossible to date), and by the early twelfth century, some scholars think, he may have been known in northern Italy and France, where names possibly derived from Arthurian folklore occur.

But it was in 1137, with the release of Geoffrey of Monmouth's *Historia Regum Britanniae,* that the legend solidified. According to Geoffrey, the *Historia* translates an ancient book in the British language. Except for his earliest readers, no one has believed him. Imaginary sources were a standard ploy of medieval writers. Nevertheless, it is not impossible that the basis of Geoffrey's work was folk history, perhaps even folk history written down. At all events, the spirit of Geoffrey's work is frankly patriotic. It gives the English and Anglo-Norman aristocracy a British hero as noble as the Norman hero Charlemagne. It traces England's genesis to the fall of Troy and the dispersion of the Trojan heroes — that misty antiquity when, for instance, Romulus fled from Troy to Rome, Tuscan to Tuscany, and Brutus to Britain — and by establishing British power as coeval with Roman and French power, it raises Britain out of its subservient position with respect to European kingdoms. This pseudo-history was accepted as fact well into the Renaissance. Arthur, the greatest of Geoffrey's mythical kings, became not only a vital symbol of British national spirit but the practical model of real medieval and Renaissance kings. Edward III, like Arthur, had a Round Table and twelve peers; Henry VII traced his claim on one side to King Arthur.

Except insofar as folk tradition continued (e.g., in the tales recorded in the much later Welsh *Mabinogion*), the further development of the Arthur legend in England was almost wholly political in impetus. Only *Sir Gawain and the Green Knight,* a few courtly tales such as Chaucer's *Wife of Bath's Tale,* and a half dozen Scottish Arthurian pieces stand outside the general trend. Wace's *Roman de Brut,* a poem in French apparently presented to the wife of Henry II of England in 1154, closely paraphrases Geoffrey and maintains the patriotic spirit, merely embellishing it with verse. Layamon's *Brut,* which began as an English paraphrase of Wace, intensifies the nationalistic spirit of the poem in three respects — first, by the use of the English language; second, by substituting native alliterative meter for Wace's continental poetic form, octosyllabic couplets; and third, by introducing new material — both new events and a new intensity of emotion — to reach more than double the length of Wace's poem; i.e., Layamon expands Wace's 1,500+ lines to 32,000+. Another English alliterative poem, the *Morte Arthure,* composed in the mid-fourteenth century, during the reign of Edward III, has political implications of a gloomier sort. Here Arthur's conquests are made to parallel Edward's, Arthur's battles grimly parody Edward's battles, and Arthur's tragedy — a fall through pride — warns Edward that a similar fate may await him. The poem is the direct source of Malory's "Arthur and King Lucius" sequence and may, in the opinion of some scholars, have provided Malory with a model for political comment through romance. Whereas the *Morte Arthure* poet identified Arthur with Edward, Malory alters details as if to equate Arthur and Henry V, suppresses the tragic conclusion of the poem, and thus perhaps sets the glory of Arthur — and of Henry V — in ironic counterpoise with what came afterward in Malory's England.

Naturally enough, the Arthurian legend reflected in Geoffrey's *Historia Regum Britanniae* was developed along very different lines in France. It provided not a national myth but subject matter for fiction. It provided material for the relatively short "Breton lays" popular in France in the mid-twelfth century and after (not all of the lays are Arthurian), and it provided themes for the more elaborate verse "romances." The earliest which have survived — and perhaps the first written — are those of Chrétien de Troyes, elegant and artificial elaborations of older Arthurian stories of (possibly) Welsh origin. Here the tales become threads for moral allegory, illustrations of virtuous behavior, courtesy, and polite conversation. Verse romances of this sort very soon became popular outside France — in Italy, Spain, Portugal, and Germany; in England the French influence resulted in the Arthurian Christian parable, *Sir Gawain and the Green Knight.*

In the twelfth and early thirteenth centuries, French verse romance gave way to prose and to still more ingenious and elaborate art. It was to this form, the prose romance, that Malory turned most often for his material. Whereas French verse romances were relatively straightforward with respect to plot, the prose romances became a gloomy medieval forest of complexity. A given romance might have dozens of main plots, hundreds of digressive episodes (indeed, main plots may be dropped and forgotten), and too many characters for the reader to keep in mind. Scholars are still uncertain about how these prose romances work, and anything we say must be speculative; but since they are Malory's point of departure, some speculation is necessary.

One thing is certain: the greatest of the prose romances—for example, the so-called Vulgate Cycle—begin by dismissing, if they ever thought of it, the Aristotelian idea that a work must be perspicuous. Like the elaborate interlace work in medieval painting, manuscript illumination, and church ornamentation, they intentionally defy intellectual comprehension. They are freighted with symbols of obscure significance, with apparently meaningful but widely separated verbal repetitions, and with subtle relationships between plots and between characters. They were written backward, so to speak, beginning with a "given" of Arthurian romance—for instance the fact that a certain knight has a certain magical sword—and explaining how the hitherto unexplained detail came about. If the prose romance form has any significance in itself, it would seem to be this: like the universe as the Christian Middle Ages conceived it, the prose romance is complex beyond all intelligibility, yet secretly ordered just as the baffling world around us is subtly ordered by God's plan. Knights go on quests, suffer more distractions, diversions, and reversals than the mind can retain; yet trifling events produce, hundreds of pages later, their destinal effects. For some of these events, the motivation of characters is carefully plotted and thoroughly explained; and though events within any given plot may be isolated by the intrusion of events from other plots, no event is isolated in the total process of the cycle's flow of reality. The seemingly shapeless form of the romance, like the devious paths its knights ride down, celebrates the optimistic doctrine that nothing is wasted, nothing lost: God moves in strange ways.

Nothing remotely resembling this art form appears in English literature. But in simplifying the French prose romances, Malory did more than reduce an incredibly complex art to mere adventure. Suppressing the carefully worked out motivations he found in his sources, dismissing some of the religious mystery, introducing a seeming realism (either dropping the magic in his sources or presenting it in flat, plain statements of what must be taken for weird fact), Malory changed the premise of Arthurian legend and gave the legend new meaning.

THE CHARACTERS

1. KING ARTHUR'S HOUSE

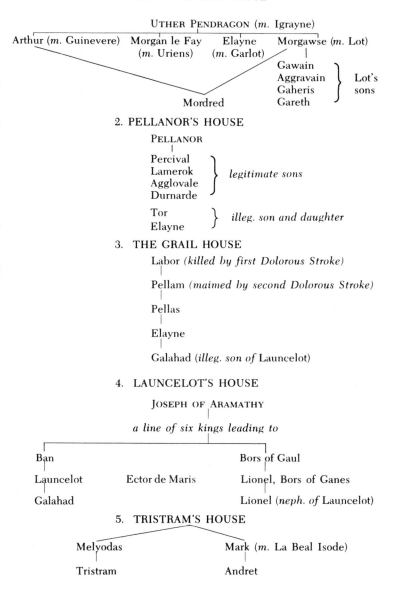

UTHER PENDRAGON (*m.* Igrayne)

Arthur (*m.* Guinevere)   Morgan le Fay   Elayne   Morgawse (*m.* Lot)
                          (*m.* Uriens)   (*m.* Garlot)

Gawain
Aggravain   } Lot's
Gaheris   } sons
Gareth

Mordred

2. PELLANOR'S HOUSE

PELLANOR

Percival
Lamerok   } *legitimate sons*
Agglovale
Durnarde

Tor   } *illeg. son and daughter*
Elayne

3. THE GRAIL HOUSE

Labor *(killed by first Dolorous Stroke)*

Pellam *(maimed by second Dolorous Stroke)*

Pellas

Elayne

Galahad *(illeg. son of* Launcelot)

4. LAUNCELOT'S HOUSE

JOSEPH OF ARAMATHY

a line of six kings leading to

Ban   Bors of Gaul

Launcelot   Ector de Maris   Lionel, Bors of Ganes

Galahad   Lionel *(neph. of* Launcelot)

5. TRISTRAM'S HOUSE

Melyodas   Mark (*m.* La Beal Isode)

Tristram   Andret

Malory's legend involves hundreds of characters whose names and family relationships, though significant, are sometimes confused. There are various reasons for this confusion in the text. Malory wrote in prison, presumably under less than ideal conditions; he used sources which were themselves sometimes obscure or confused; he consistently changed certain names for purposes of his own but occasionally let the name found in the source creep in; he sometimes misunderstood his French sources; he left no perfect copy of his work—we have only Caxton's much edited edition and one scribal manuscript riddled with errors. The accompanying chart of major character relationships may be helpful.

Other important characters include Merlin the magician, a devil's son; the Lady of the Lake, from whom Arthur gets his sword; Nineve, the sorceress who becomes Lady of the Lake after the death of the first one; Balyn and Balan, the cursed brothers whose relics go to Launcelot and Galahad; Tarquin and Bereuse Saunz Pité, enemies of knighthood. Palomydes, Tristram's rival for La Beal Isode, is sometimes designated as the son of Asclabor, elsewhere as "next of kin" to Pellanor. His function in the tragedy is clearer than his genealogy: the destructive potential in his adulterous goal comments on the loves of Tristram and Launcelot, and his pact of friendship with Pellanor's sons (who may or may not be his close relatives) links him with the feud which will wreck Arthur's kingdom.

All of the major houses charted are torn by deadly rivalries and undermined by adulterous love. Arthur and King Lot, his brother-in-law, are enemies partly because of the incestuous union of Arthur and Lot's wife Morgawse—the union which produces Mordred—and Arthur and Lot also begin as rivals for the throne of England. Arthur's best knight, Launcelot, is lover to his wife. Similarly, Melyodas and Mark are political rivals, and Mark's best knight, Tristram, is lover to his wife Isode. Pellanor, fighting for Arthur and the unity of his kingdom, kills Lot and sets off the feud between his own house and Lot's, a feud destined to destroy the kingdom. Yet, ironically, the Grail curse is ended when two rival houses—the house which brought

Christ's relics over and the house which received the Dolorous
Strokes—are adulterously brought together to produce Galahad.

SUMMARIES AND COMMENTARIES

Since *Le Morte Darthur* is long and difficult, it is impossible
to give equal emphasis to all parts of the work in the space available here; at the same time, since the legend is coherent, every
part having its vital function (or so most recent critics believe),
it is impossible simply to drop sections out and still make sense
of the whole. For these reasons it will be necessary to hurry over
certain sections with only the most general kind of summary
and sometimes to postpone any commentary until the end of a
group of related sections of the work.

I. THE TALE OF KING ARTHUR

1. Merlin

The mighty king of all primeval England, Uther Pendragon,
lusts after Igrayne, wife of the Duke of Cornwall. Uther invites
the duke and his wife to his castle and propositions her. She
refuses him, tells her husband, and the duke and Igrayne slip
out of Uther's castle by night and flee. On the advice of his
knights, the king, sick with lust and rage, marches on the Duke
of Cornwall. While the siege is still on, Merlin the magician
arranges a pact with King Uther. He will transform Uther into
the image of the duke and get him to bed with Igrayne. The
condition is that the child who will be conceived on this night
shall go to Merlin for rearing as he sees fit.

The child is conceived hours after the real duke's death,
and King Uther later marries the widow. On the same morning,
by King Uther's request, two fellow kings—Lot and Nantres—
marry two of Uther's daughters, and the third daughter, Morgan
le Fay, is put to school in a nunnery and becomes a necro-
mancer; she later marries King Uriens. The child is born and
delivered unchristened to Merlin.

Two years pass. In this time Uther's enemies strike at him repeatedly, killing many of his people. Uther falls sick, and in the hour of his death, Merlin gets him to proclaim his son Arthur the future king of England.

After Uther's death, the kingdom is in jeopardy, every baron struggling to seize control. Merlin goes to the Archbishop of Canterbury, tells him a miracle is coming soon and advises him to assemble all the lords of the kingdom at Christmas. They come and find a sword lodged in a stone, and on it the legend: *Whoso pulleth out this sword from this stone and anvil is duly born King of all England.* No man can budge it, and to keep them in hand, the archbishop arranges a New Year's Day tournament. To this tournament a knight of low station, Sir Ector, comes with his son Kay and the child Merlin placed in his care, Arthur.

On the way, Kay loses his sword and sends Arthur back. Arthur brings the sword from the stone. When they hear of this, the barons are outraged at the thought of being ruled by a boy. They postpone their decision on Arthur's kingship again and again but at last accept it, at the urging of the commons, and Arthur is crowned. He redistributes the land, redresses old wrongs, and extends his realm, in a few years bringing all the North, Scotland, and Wales to submission.

Arthur has himself crowned in Wales and the mightiest kings of his time come to the coronation, among them King Lot, King Nantres, and King Uriens, the husbands of Uther's three daughters. Arthur is pleased, thinking they come from love and respect; but the gifts he sends them are scornfully refused: they have come to fight him. With 500 men, Arthur withdraws to a tower, and Merlin goes to talk with the hostile kings. He tells them of Arthur's lineage and arranges a parley, then vanishes from their midst and returns to Arthur. He tells Arthur to answer his enemies boldly, for destiny is on his side.

The parley fails, war begins, and with the help of his magical sword Excalibur, gleaming in his enemies' eyes like twenty torches, Arthur routs his enemies. He returns to London, and there Merlin gives him a three-part plan of war. First he advises that Arthur get help from two kings over the sea, Ban and Bors, and that Arthur promise in return to help with their wars. Second, he advises a midnight attack on the greatest and bravest of Arthur's enemies, King Lot. Third, he advises that the armies of Ban and Bors be moved secretly into the English forest of Bedgraine. This Merlin himself accomplishes. Arthur and his army fight the hostile kings — grown to a league of eleven — and bring the battle to a draw. When the enemy is weakened and weary, the fresh armies of Ban and Bors descend.

King Lot and his allies are badly beaten and might be destroyed, but Merlin tells Arthur to quit or Fortune will turn on him. The hostile armies will not trouble him now for three years. Arthur and his allies stop, joyful over their success, and Merlin sees that all that happened in the battle is written down. An interlude of peace follows: a seemingly irrational joke by Merlin, then the appearance of an earl's daughter on whom Arthur gets a child who will become, later, a Round Table knight.

Now Arthur, Ban, and Bors go to help King Lodegreaunce with his war and win it for him. There Arthur first sees Guinevere and immediately loves her. Ban and Bors return home, and so do the eleven hostile kings, who find their lands overrun with Saracens and other bandits — lands Arthur would have protected for them, they realize, if they had not struggled against him. They drive out the Saracens and begin to plot vengeance for the battle of Bedgraine.

Arthur goes to Carlyon, where the wife of King Lot and his four sons — Gawain, Gaheris, Aggravain, and Gareth — come to visit, actually to spy. Unaware that Lot's wife is his own sister, Arthur gets a child on her — Mordred. That night Arthur dreams that his land is overrun by gryphons and serpents which burn the land and slay the people; he fights them in his dream and, with great difficulty, slays them. To drive the nightmare out of his mind, Arthur goes hunting. He chases a hart until his horse falls dead. A yeoman brings another horse, but Arthur sits lost in thought, near a fountain. A mysterious beast comes, drinks, and moves on; immediately afterward a strange knight comes — Sir Pellanor, hunter of the Questing Beast. Arthur offers to take up the quest, but Sir Pellanor says that destiny will allow none but him or his next of kin to kill the beast; then he takes Arthur's horse by force.

Then Merlin comes, disguised as a child of fourteen. Merlin tells Arthur that he is Uther's son by Igrayne. Arthur refuses to believe the boy because of his youth, and Merlin leaves, then returns as an old man. He now tells Arthur that if he would only have listened to him, the boy might have told him many things. Merlin-as-old-man tells him only that he has lain by his sister and has gotten on her the child who will destroy him. Then, revealing himself, Merlin prophesies that whereas Arthur will die a worshipful death, Merlin's death will be shameful — he will be sealed in the earth alive.

A few days later a squire comes to the court with his dying master, wounded by Sir Pellanor. A young squire of Arthur's court, Gryfflet, asks to be made knight and avenge the wrong; and against Merlin's advice, Arthur grants the boy's request. Gryfflet fights Pellanor and returns again to the court nearly dead. With his mind on Gryfflet, Arthur hastily and angrily dismisses envoys from King Lucius of Rome and rides out himself — again against Merlin's advice — fights Pellanor, and is beaten. He is about to be beheaded when Merlin saves him by means of a spell. Merlin tells him that Pellanor will do him great service later, and that his two sons, Percival and Lamerok of Wales, will be two of the most valiant knights of the Round Table.

Having lost his sword in the fight with Pellanor, Arthur asks Merlin what he should do. Merlin guides him to a magical lake where an arm reaches out of the water holding a sword. Merlin takes him now to the Lady of the Lake, who gives him the sword, demanding that he give some return gift later, when she asks for it. Arthur agrees. The sword is the finest in the world, the scabbard better yet: as long as he wears the scabbard, nothing can harm him.

They return to court, where new troubles are waiting. Messengers from King Royns of North Wales say that Royns has overcome the eleven kings, has taken their beards, and now demands Arthur's. Arthur refuses them as angrily as he earlier refused the Roman king's demand for tribute. Then, advised by Merlin that he should destroy all highborn children delivered on May Day, because Mordred is one of them, Arthur orders these children brought to his court. They are put on a ship, which drives onto rocks killing all but one — Mordred. Many of Arthur's lords and barons are furious, hearing of the death of their sons. Some blame Arthur, some Merlin. But for the time they hold their peace.

Commentary

Besides straightening out and tightening the development of plot, Malory departs from his source for "Merlin" in two main ways: in the characterization of Arthur, King Lot, and Merlin, and in his grouping of tribute demands at the end of this episode. The effectiveness of the characterization is partly a product of Malory's style — his swift presentation of action, his blunt realism, his habit of avoiding any complicated analysis of emotion. For example:

> So whan the duke and his wyf were comyn unto the kynge, by the meanes of grete lordes they were accorded bothe. The kynge lyked and loved this lady wel, and he made them grete chere out of mesure and desyred to have lyen by her, but she was a passyng good woman and wold not assente unto the kynge.

When the duke and his wife have retreated and the siege is underway, Malory says:

> Thenne for pure angre and for grete love of fayr Igrayne the kyng Uther felle seke. So came to the kynge Uther syre Ulfius, a noble knyght, and asked the kynge why he was seke.
> "I shall telle the," said the kynge. "I am seke for angre and for love of fayre Igrayne, that I may not be hool."
> "Well, my lord," said syre Ulfius, "I shal seke Merlyn and he shalle do yow remedy, that youre herte shal be pleasyd."

By these swift strokes, Malory arrives at the introduction of Merlin, agent of Arthur's rise and fall. On the other hand, Malory can switch from swift narration to scenes slowly and carefully worked out. When Arthur draws the sword from the stone, for instance, Kay's lie (his pretense that he himself drew it out), his father's suspicion, Arthur's grief at finding he is not Sir Ector's son, and Arthur's pledge that he will always be faithful to Ector and Kay, are all developed slowly, through dialog and gesture.

But at the heart of Malory's characterization is his original sense of how each character contributes to and defines the total tragedy. He makes Merlin directly responsible for every step of Arthur's progress — even his birth. He seems at first to be a prophet, a direct agent of God. But he is not. He is part demonic tempter, part wizard: he knows necromancy, and he can see into the future, but his vision, like that of any astrologer or (as Lot says) "dream-reader" is imperfect. In medieval terms, he can see into the workings of Fortune but not always into those of Providence. To trust him is to trust not God but "the World."

Malory's method is to present Merlin first in his best light — manipulating Uther's lust to his own end, guiding Arthur to greater and greater power — then to reveal, little by little, Merlin's dangerous flaws. In the joke he plays on Arthur after the battle of Bedgraine, Merlin appears dressed in the hides of black sheep and offers treasure "under the ground" for a gift from Arthur. Nothing comes of the joke, but it has ominous overtones of demonic temptation. For medieval writers, to trust in the World (whose prophet is Merlin) is to trust the devil, emblematically identified with both black sheep and treasure under the ground. (We learn later that Merlin is a devil's son.) Merlin's deadly mistakes — his failure to warn Arthur against lying with Lot's wife and his still more terrible mistake in the attempted murder of Mordred — reveal how dangerous his limitations are.

Malory's King Lot is a much more heroic and forceful figure than the King Lot of the sources. Malory focuses on him at once, makes him the leader of Arthur's enemies, and insists on his nobility and courage (for instance, Lot's nightmare and panic in the sources is assigned to another king in Malory). He is thus made a worthy antagonist to Merlin's plan and Arthur's kingship. And Arthur is similarly ennobled: Malory underscores his loyalty to Sir Ector, to kings who are his friends, and to the young squire Gryfflet.

The structure of the "Merlin" is as remarkable as the characterization. Half-way through, events flow in a straight narrative line, reflecting our sense that all is well; Merlin is in full control. But immediately after Merlin's joke, everything changes. Apparently motivated by casual lust, Arthur sleeps with an earl's daughter and gets on her a son who will do him great honor. Immediately afterward, in what seems to Arthur an exactly similar situation, he commits incest and dooms himself.

All the remaining incidents involve demands for tribute, one after another—Sir Pellanor's demands, King Lucius' demand, King Royns' demand for Arthur's beard. All the demands are stalled off for the moment, but they are all still there, biding their time like the fathers of the murdered children. Thus the opening tale, "Merlin," sets up the ironic principle which will govern the whole *Morte Darthur*.

2. The Knight with the Two Swords

After King Arthur hears of the crimes of King Royns of North Wales, he calls the knights from all his lands to a general council at Camelot. When the council is assembled, there comes a damsel sent by the Lady Lyle of Avilon. Under her mantle the damsel has a sword which is fixed in its scabbard and cannot be drawn out except by a knight completely pure of heart. It is her curse that she must wear the cumbersome sword and scabbard everywhere she goes. Arthur and all his knights try to draw the sword and fail. At last, a prisoner among them, Sir Balyn, newly released from the dungeon and shabbily dressed, asks that he be allowed to try, for though he has been accused of a crime, and though his apparel is humble, he believes himself worthy. He draws the sword out easily, making some of the other knights fiercely jealous, and he says he will keep it, even though it is a fated sword: it will murder his dearest friend. Arthur apologizes for misjudging and mistreating Balyn, a man proved so noble.

Balyn accepts the apology and prepares to leave the court. Before he has left, the Lady of the Lake arrives and demands the gift Arthur promised her when she gave him his sword. She wants either Sir Balyn's head or that of the damsel who gave him his sword. Arthur refuses, and Balyn, recognizing her as his mother's murderer, hacks off her head. Arthur is outraged — as a visitor to the court she was in his safekeeping — and says he will never forgive Balyn for this murder. Balyn leaves and resolves to kill the tyrant King Royns and thus win back Arthur's respect. Sir Launceor of Ireland, one of Arthur's knights whom Balyn's success has humiliated, asks permission to ride after Balyn and avenge the Lady of the Lake; Arthur, still angry, grants it.

Now Merlin arrives and reveals the history of the sword. The damsel who brought it once loved a knight who was slain by her brother. She took the lover's sword to the Lady of Avilon and asked her help. With witchly whimsy, the Lady of Avilon sealed the sword in the scabbard so that only the best and hardiest man in the kingdom would be able to draw it, and with it he would slay not *her* brother but his own. Merlin reprimands the damsel for bringing the sword here, knowing its curse.

Launceor of Ireland now sets out after Balyn. They fight, Balyn kills him by accident, and Launceor's lady takes his sword and brandishes it. Balyn tries to get the sword away from her but cannot without hurting her wrist. When he lets go, she kills herself with it. Balyn is shocked and grieved at this needless waste and hurries away. He meets his beloved brother Balan, tells him all that has happened, and agrees to let him join the hunt for King Royns. A great king comes by and asks who killed Launceor. Balyn tells him, and the king predicts that Launceor's relatives will want vengeance. The king reveals that he is King

Mark (a vicious double-dealer later in Malory), then encamps to bury the bodies as befits their station.

Merlin appears and tells King Mark that in this burial spot will one day be fought the greatest battle ever fought between two knights who dearly love one another—Launcelot du Lake and Tristram. Merlin will not tell Mark his name, but on the day Tristram is taken with his lady, then Merlin will give both his name and news King Mark will be sorry to hear. Then Merlin tells Balyn that because he let this lady die (though he could not prevent it) he is fated to strike "the Dolorous Stroke," a stroke more terrible than any but that which killed Christ. Balyn does not believe him. If he thought he were capable of such an act, Balyn says, he would kill himself on the spot. Merlin vanishes. Balyn and Balan take their leave of King Mark, Balyn identifying himself as The Knight with the Two Swords.

As the brothers ride on, Merlin appears in disguise and shows them where King Royns is. They kill his attendants, wound him badly, and send him to Arthur. Merlin reveals that the knight who captured Royns was Balyn, and again Arthur repents his hasty judgment of Balyn. Merlin says that Royns' brother Nero will come with a great host tomorrow for vengeance and Arthur prepares. Then, to give Arthur's army a chance, Merlin goes to Nero's ally, King Lot, and holds him with tales of prophecy until it is too late for him to help Nero. Balan and Balyn join Arthur's forces and fight brilliantly. A messenger tells Lot what has happened—Arthur has easily destroyed Nero and his forces and is now in a position to destroy King Lot. Lot is furious at Merlin's trick but will not accept terms from Arthur because of Arthur's seduction of Lot's wife.

As for Merlin, he is grieved that Lot must die, but he has known from the start that in this battle it must either be Lot or King Arthur. Sir Pellanor, the Knight of the Questing Beast, kills Lot, for which deed he will later be killed himself by Lot's son Gawain. Lot's forces flee and Arthur buries Lot, Nero, and the twelve kings who supported them. Merlin adorns the tombs with symbolic figures and tells Arthur more of what is to come.

He warns that he will not remain with Arthur long and that Arthur must guard his magical scabbard carefully, for the woman he trusts most will steal it from him. Arthur gives the scabbard to his sister Morgan le Fay for safekeeping, and she gives it to her lover Accolon. Merlin tells, too, of the battle of Salisbury, against Mordred.

After these revelations, Arthur lies sick and heavy with thought. A moaning knight rides by, and Arthur sends Balyn to bring him back. Balyn brings the knight, parting him from his lady, and as they approach Arthur's pavilion the moaning knight is murdered by a knight named Garlon, who is invisible. Balyn returns to the dead knight's lady, taking over his quest. Another knight joins them and is similarly slain by the invisible knight. They bury him and on his stone appears a prophecy of Gawain's vengeance on Pellanor.

Balyn and the damsel ride on, come to a castle, and Balyn enters. A gate drops, separating him from his lady, and men set on her as if to kill her. Balyn climbs a tower, leaps a wall to help her, and learns that in this castle every passing maiden is bled, for a dishful of some maiden's blood will cure the sick lady of the castle. Balyn bleeds the maiden himself, without harming her, but the blood is not pure enough—only that of Percival's sister will do, and she will die giving it.

Now Balyn is directed to King Pellam's castle, where he will find Garlon. Balyn kills Garlon before Pellam's eyes, and Pellam fights to avenge his brother. Losing his sword, Balyn takes a marvelous spear and strikes with that. The castle falls to the earth, all but Pellam and Balyn are killed, and the land goes to waste. Balyn has struck the Dolorous Stroke. Merlin rouses Balyn and tells him that Pellam will not be whole until Galahad heals him in the Grail Quest, for this is the country where Joseph of Aramathy brought "parte of the bloode of oure Lorde...," and the spear is the one that killed Christ.

Balyn parts from Merlin and rides grieving through the Wasteland. When he has passed out of it he comes upon a knight who grieves because his lady has missed her assignation. Balyn helps the knight find the lady—sleeping in an ugly knight's arms. In a rage, the jealous lover strikes off their heads as they sleep, then mourns worse than before, for he has killed what he loved best; then he kills himself. Again Balyn is to blame.

Miserable, Balyn rides on and comes to a castle where he is told he must fight a knight who guards an island of ladies. One of the knights of the castle lends Balyn a shield better than his own. Balyn fights the guardian of the island in order to pass, and because Balyn does not have his usual shield, the island guardian —Balyn's brother—does not recognize him. They wound each other mortally, but before he dies Balyn learns that if he had won and lived, it would have been little better. Because Balan killed the earlier keeper of the island, he has been bound to take over his position, which would now have fallen to Balyn.

The brothers are buried in a single grave, and around the tomb, partly with the doomed brothers' relics—their swords and scabbards—Merlin sets up events of the future. He sets a new pommel on Balyn's cursed sword, and now no man can handle it but Launcelot or Galahad, and with this sword Launcelot will kill his dearest friend, Gawain. He leaves Balyn's scabbard for Galahad to find, and he puts Balyn's sword into a floating stone to be attained by Galahad.

Commentary

"The Knight with the Two Swords" is an ingenious and complex development of the two closing motifs of the "Merlin." In the first place, "The Knight with the Two Swords" focuses on the ironic destinal forces which Merlin can only in part control. Trusting in God and in "adventure"—or Fortune—Balyn takes the sword that is rightfully his. He knows himself to be pure in heart—his winning of the sword proves it—and so he cannot believe he will kill the man he loves best. Neither can he believe, later, that he will strike the Dolorous Stroke. He does both. Moreover, every pure and good cause he undertakes results in catastrophe: in his self-defense against Launceor of

Ireland he causes the death of the knight, and in his wish not to hurt the wrist of Launceor's lady he allows her the chance to commit suicide. So it is with all he does. Even in striking the Dolorous Stroke he acts without guilt, unaware of the consequences. His limitation is simply that he is mortal—non-omniscient—and the limitation is underscored after every mistake either by the appearance of magic writing or by Merlin's prediction, through his greater foreknowledge, of what later catastrophes will come in these same places, perhaps as direct or indirect results of Balyn's actions.

The second motif developed from the end of the "Merlin" is that of vengeance. Every detail Malory has brought together from his widely scattered sources involves vengeance (usually as family revenge) or its ironic inversion, intentional or accidental betrayal by a member of the family or by a lover. In each case, the vengeance or betrayal of love is unpredictable for ordinary men. The damsel who carried her lover's sword to the Lady of Avilon could not know that, for mysterious reasons of her own, the witch would turn it into an instrument of monstrous harm. Arthur could not know, in sending Launceor after Balyn, that in acting on his own outrage (coupled with Launceor's jealousy) he would trigger far greater wrongs. Nor could Balyn know that in pursuing King Royns he would rouse King Nero.

It is through Arthur's war with Lot, Nero, and the eleven kings that Arthur's kingdom is unified, but this unity is grounded on the same principle of violence that operates in personal feuds, weaving an ever more intricate web of revenge and betrayal and debt. Once begun, the process cannot be turned back. While men exact payment of an eye for an eye, both the ministers of Fate (the Lady of the Lake and, sometimes, Merlin) and also the design of Providence strike out at petty acts of violence with terrifying force. If the purest and most just of men can be destroyed in this process—that is, Balyn—the fault must lie in the chivalric code itself, if anywhere. And yet it is the code which, with Merlin's help, establishes Arthur's rule of order. Without civilized order and the redressing of wrongs, the world could have no defense against tyrants like Royns, outlaws like Garlon, men of desperate need, such as the blood thieves of the sick lady's castle, or cruel faithlessness (e.g., Morgan). The chivalric code is founded, in short, on deadly paradox.

3. Tor and Pellanor

At the request of his lords, who are concerned about Arthur's founding a royal line, Arthur marries Guinevere—against Merlin's advice. As dowery, her father Laudegreaunce gives Arthur the Round Table. Merlin gathers knights to fill as many of the 150 seats as he can. Arthur dubs two young knights, Lot's son Gawain and the bastard son of Sir Pellanor. At the wedding feast, each of the two new knights, along with Sir Pellanor, get knightly work to do.

A white hart runs into the hall, pursued by black hounds. A disgrunted knight, knocked down by the hart, seizes a hound and rides away with it. A lady appears, says the hound is hers, and asks that some knight pursue the thief. A strange knight rides in, seizes the obstreperous lady, and takes her away by force. King Arthur is pleased to be rid of her, but Merlin warns that these wrongs must be redressed if his court is to be respected. Arthur orders Gawain after the hart, Sir Tor after the knight and hound, and Sir Pellanor after the kidnaper and the kidnaped lady. The remainder of the tale treats the three knights' adventures.

Gawain comes honorably out of two encounters, impartially judging the conflict of two brothers and disinterestedly overcoming a knight who guards a waterway. But in his third fight he is not impartial: to avenge his murdered hounds he refuses mercy to the knight he overcomes. A lady throws herself over the knight to save him and Gawain accidentally cuts off her head. He will carry this shame until his death. Four knights come to avenge the lady and, in contrast to Gawain, show mercy when ladies ask it in his behalf. Gawain returns to court, and Guinevere imposes his penance.

Sir Tor, pursuing the hound, encounters two knights served by a dwarf, fights them at their demand, beats them, and gives them mercy when they ask it. The dwarf leads Tor to the hound and Tor seizes it; but as he returns to Arthur's court a knight demands the hound. They fight, Tor overcomes the knight, and the knight refuses to ask for mercy. A lady rides up and asks a gift. Tor agrees, and the lady asks for the wounded knight's head. He murdered her brother and would show no mercy, though the lady pleaded for half an hour on her knees. The wounded knight now asks mercy, but because he asks too late, Tor grants the lady's request. Tor returns to Camelot and is honored both by the court and by Merlin.

Sir Pellanor, riding on his quest of the kidnaper, passes a lady with a wounded knight in her arms, who asks for his help. In his haste, he refuses to stop. He achieves his quest nobly, but on his return he finds that both the lady he would not help and her wounded protector have been eaten by lions. Back at Camelot, Guinevere reproaches Pellanor for these deaths, and Pellanor crossly shrugs it off: the lady should have taken care of herself. Merlin tells Pellanor that the lady was his own daughter and that his act was shameful. Because Pellanor would not stop to help the lady, his best friend shall fail him at need. This is the penance God has ordained, he says. Arthur distributes lands and rewards, then spells out the new code of the Round Table, which requires them to show mercy, to fight for the right, and to honor ladies.

Commentary

Like all titles in Malory, including *Le Morte Darthur* itself, the misleading title "Tor and Pellanor" is not by Malory but by later editors. In this tale the chivalric code, found wanting in the preceding tale of Balyn, is modified. It is most obviously modified, of course, by the adventures of the three knights. The code must be merciful, as all the tales show; and the code insists that a knight must stop if he possibly can for any person in distress. The code is also modified in more subtle ways. The three adventures take place within the framing tale of Arthur's wedding, an event also significant with respect to the code.

For Arthur's knights, Guinevere represents the stability of rule which comes from the founding of a legitimate line of succession. As judge of the knights' adventures she also serves as the court spokesman for *love*. She imposes on Gawain the penance of special devotion to mercy (a check against the law of revenge) and special service to ladies (i.e., the beautiful and defenseless). She approves Sir Tor, whose charity and respect for ladies is flawless. It is she who condemns Sir Pellanor for failing to save a lady's life when he might have — and her "civilized" judgment is sealed by a judgment from, in effect, God.

Finally, the tale contrasts the ideal of legitimate lineage affirmed in Arthur's marriage, public and lawful, with the kind of lineage achieved by Sir Pellanor. Pellanor's bastard son Sir Tor, raised by a cowherd, must advance without the help his father owes him. Pellanor's daughter dies because her father did not know her. But legitimacy too raises problems. Gawain, legitimate son of Lot, longs for vengeance on Pellanor, his father's slayer. His brother persuades him not to strike yet, but he will, sooner or later. Knowing who one's father is — and who it is that killed him — can make mercy an unattainable ideal.

4. The Death of Merlin and the War with the Five Kings
5. Arthur and Accolon   6. Gawain, Ywain, and Marhault

In the first of these interrelated tales, Merlin falls dotingly in love with the maiden Sir Pellanor brought into court, Nineve. She is afraid to lie with Merlin because he is a devil's son, and in his company she is "ever passynge wery of him," but she hides her disgust in order to learn the secrets of his art. She travels with him to the court of Sir Ban, where Merlin predicts fame for Ban's son Launcelot. Afterward, through magic, Nineve seals Merlin in a cave.

Meanwhile, Arthur goes to war against a league of five kings. Since Arthur leaves for war in haste, in advance of his allies, the enemy has the advantage; but by pure luck, Arthur, Kay, Gawain, and Gryfflet encounter the five kings alone. Gawain advises flight, but Kay vows he'll kill two of the kings, evening the odds, and does so. Arthur and the other knights kill the remainder, and Guinevere gives Kay her formal and characteristic praise: he is well worthy of some lady's love.

The host of the five kings is easily destroyed, and the eight Round Table knights who die in this action are replaced. One of the knights elevated to Round Table status is Tor. At his advancement another minor knight, Sir Bagdemagus, is angry. He leaves the court, resolving not to return until he has proved his worth. He finds a sign of the Grail — evidence that he is right in his judgment of himself — and later finds the cave where Merlin is sealed up alive. Merlin tells him that no one but Nineve can free him, and Bagdemagus rides on.

The second tale treats Morgan le Fay's attempted murder of Arthur. Riding in pursuit of a great hart, Arthur, Accolon, and King Uriens come upon an enchanted barge, where they are given a feast, then shown to splendid beds. Through Morgan's magic, Morgan's husband, King Uriens, awakens in his wife's arms; Accolon, her beloved, awakens at the edge of an enchanted well; and Arthur awakens in the dungeon of the cowardly King Damas, who imprisons and starves errant knights in hopes of forcing one to fight for him against his brother, an honorable king of whom Damas is jealous.

Arthur agrees to fight for Damas in order to free the other knights. As Damas's overlord, he can punish him later. Meanwhile Accolon is given Arthur's sword and scabbard by Morgan, who loves him and hopes to make him king and herself his queen. She arranges it that Accolon fights for Damas's brother. Thus Accolon and Arthur fight, neither one knowing the other, with magic on Accolon's side. Nineve, knowing Morgan's plan, comes to Arthur's aid and he is able to defeat Accolon. Accolon dies a few days later.

Morgan, supposing Arthur dead, raises a sword to kill her husband in his sleep, but her son Ywain prevents the murder. Morgan steals back the magic scabbard Arthur has gotten from Accolon, and when Arthur pursues her she throws it in a lake. She meets Accolon's cousin, who is about to be executed on the charge of having seduced a knight's wife. She rescues him, murders the cuckolded husband, and makes Accolon's cousin (Manessen) her new defender.

In the third tale, Morgan sends a peace offering to Arthur — a mantle wrought of jewels. He is impressed but says nothing. Nineve, the Damsel of the Lake, advises him to ask the messenger from Morgan to put on the mantle herself. When she is forced to do so, the messenger bursts into flame and burns to ashes. In his fury Arthur banishes Morgan's son Ywain, suspecting him of complicity. Gawain leaves with him — "for whoso banyshyth my cosyn jarmayne shall banyshe me."

As Gawain and Ywain ride through a forest they find twelve maidens spitting on a white shield. When they ask what this means, the maidens explain that the shield belongs to the knight Marhault, a man who scorns all women. Marhault draws near, and Ywain and Gawain fight him. When he has overcome them both he does not kill them but tells them that he has been falsely accused. The twelve maidens are enchantresses. The three knights resolve to ride together.

In the mysterious country of Arroy they find a fountain and three damsels, one old, one middle-aged, one young. The three damsels are here, they say, to guide errant knights to adventure. Each knight must choose a lady and ride with her for a year. Ywain takes the oldest, Marhault takes the next, and Gawain takes the youngest. Then each knight goes his separate way with his guide.

Sir Gawain is quickly abandoned by his lady: he avoids a fight she advises him to take upon himself. When later he does help the knight he was earlier advised to help, he betrays his trust. He tells the knight, Sir Pellas (son of the maimed king,

Pellam), that he will win the love of his haughty lady for him; but Gawain lies with her instead. Pellas is tempted to kill Gawain for his treachery, but at last he merely leaves a sign that he knows, then retires. Nineve avenges Sir Pellas by forcing his disdainful lady to dote on him and by freeing Pellas of his passion for her. By yet another spell, Nineve makes Pellas her own lover and they live together happily.

Marhault, riding with the middle-aged lady, avenges wrongs as a true knight should. He meets a duke who is a sworn enemy to King Arthur's court because Gawain long ago murdered the duke's seventh son. Marhault fights the duke and his remaining six sons, beats them, and gets their vow to drop the feud. Marhault fights afterward in a great tournament and wins the same prize Pellas won in another tournament. Finally, he fights a giant for the Earl of Fergus and destroys him.

Ywain, riding with the oldest damsel, wins a tournament prize (as did Pellas and Marhault), then fights two cowardly knights who have taken land by "extortion" — or seizure. Ywain wins the fight but is so badly hurt that it takes him half a year to recover.

The three knights of Arthur's court come together again and learn that Arthur has repented of banishing Ywain. On the day of Pentecost — the day on which Arthur's knights each year renew their vow to live by Arthur's code — Gawain, Ywain, and Marhault, as well as Sir Pellas and Nineve, return to Camelot. Pellas and Marahult take first and second place, respectively, at Arthur's tournament, and for this, and also for their year's deeds, are honored by appointment to the Round Table. Only for love of Arthur does Pellas spare Gawain. He takes pleasure all the rest of his life in shaming Gawain at tournaments.

Commentary

These three tales are developed together, without closing summaries or new beginnings, and thus must certainly have been intended to form a unit — a single episodic tale. (Cf. the opening and closing summaries of all other tales discussed thus far.) At all events, their interrelationship is obvious. Nineve the Damsel of the Lake figures prominently in all three: it is she who seals Merlin in the earth alive, she who saves Arthur in the fight with Accolon, and she who saves and rewards Pellas after Gawain's betrayal. She seems to represent, in effect, combined prudence and loyalty.

Sir Gawain figures in the first and third tales. He offers cowardly, though not disloyal, advice in the first tale when he advises Arthur to flee the five kings, since the fight will be five against four. In the third tale his cowardly and disloyal behavior contrasts with the behavior of Pellas, Marhault, and Ywain, all of whom fight for the right against heavy odds. (Gawain refuses a fight against multiple opponents, though his guide advises it; he enters no tournaments; and he betrays his trust both to a fellow knight and to a lady.)

All three tales centrally concern love-betrayal — Nineve's justifiable betrayal of Merlin; Accolon's unwitting yet consenting betrayal of Arthur and Morgan's thoroughly treacherous betrayal of both Arthur and Uriens; and, in the third tale, Gawain's betrayal of Pellas and his lady. These central betrayals occur within a pattern of lesser love-betrayals and refusals of love. Together, then, the three tales establish in dramatic terms the qualities of right and wrong love, or, more precisely, of true love, prudent or imprudent, versus jealous love, good or bad. Merlin's infatuation balances that of Pellas; Morgan's vicious love of Accolon balances Gawain's vicious lust; Pellas' nobly restrained jealousy parallels Bagdemagus' nobly restrained jealousy in another sphere and plays ironically against Gawain's jealous blood-loyalty to Ywain.

II. ARTHUR AND KING LUCIUS

Emperor Lucius of Rome sends messengers to Arthur's court demanding tribute. Though Arthur is furious, he controls himself and takes council with his knights. Sir Cador is delighted with the possibility of honorable war; the King of Wales vows vengeance on the Viscount of Rome, who once treated him shamefully; the young Launcelot du Lake eagerly offers his aid; and the remaining knights also pledge their full support. Arthur gives the envoys of Rome their answer and they leave. They warn Lucius of Arthur's might, but Lucius attacks nevertheless, supported by giants and Saracens. He takes the lands Arthur won from King Claudas and moves toward Normandy. Arthur leaves his kingdom in the hands of two noblemen and Guinevere, and, though his wife swoons from grief, prepares to embark. If he dies, Constantine, Cador's son, is to succeed him.

On his ship Arthur dreams of a battle between a dragon and a huge bear. According to his dream interpreter, the dragon represents Arthur himself; the bear is either some tyrant or a giant he will destroy. As soon as he lands at Normandy he hears of a giant who torments the land, murders women and children, and has recently stolen a duchess, wife to Arthur's cousin. Arthur calls Kay and Bedivere and tells them to arm themselves; they will go with him on a pilgrimage to St. Michael's Mount, "where mervayles are shewed."

They ride through a beautiful countryside full of birds, then alight. Arthur says he will seek the "saint" alone. He finds the grave of the duchess, beside it an old woman who warns him that the giant has no respect for treaties. He will accept nothing from Arthur but Guinevere. Arthur fights the giant, kills him, and jokes more with Bedivere and Kay on this "saint" he has found. He gives away the giant's treasure, attributes the victory to God, and moves on.

Word comes that Lucius is fairly close, and Arthur sends King Bors and Gawain to warn Lucius that he must withdraw. A knight at Lucius' court, Sir Gaius, mocks Gawain, and Gawain—quick-tempered and vengeful as ever—cuts off Gaius' head. The two knights flee; the Romans pursue; Gawain and Bors are forced to turn and fight. They drive the foremost Romans back, and as the Romans withdraw, Round Table knights burst from ambush and destroy Romans on every side. In this fight Sir Bors and Sir Berell are captured. Gawain, furious at this indignity, breaks through the Roman ranks and, with a younger knight's help, rescues his friends.

Throughout the battle Gawain fights nobly, taking highborn prisoners and enduring painful wounds. When he and the others return to Arthur's hall, Arthur greets him eagerly and says he would give him the prisoners' heads if he thought it would help his wounds. Gawain graciously dismisses the half-offer. Then Arthur sends the prisoners to Paris for incarceration, with Sir Cador and Launcelot at the head of the expedition.

Launcelot and Cador meet an ambush of Romans. The British force is small and weak, but the older knights make knights of their squires and fight heroically. In the end, largely through Launcelot's incredible fighting ability, the Romans are overwhelmed, nearly all of them being killed. The British return to Arthur and report the victory and their own minor losses. Arthur condemns the battle as foolhardy, but Launcelot insists that to turn back even when overmatched would be shameful, and his fellow knights support him.

The Romans who make it back to Lucius beg him to drop his hopeless war against Arthur. Lucius scoffs and launches a new attack. In this battle the Welsh king fulfills his vow to destroy the Viscount of Rome, Launcelot steals Lucius' banner, and all the other great knights — Cador, Kay, Gawain, Bors, Pellas, Marhault, and others — fight better than ever before "syn God made the worlde." Sir Kay and Sir Bedivere are wounded, almost mortally, and now Arthur fights more fiercely than ever. Meanwhile Gawain and Launcelot fight splendidly, side by side. Arthur now forbids any taking of prisoners: in vengeance for Sir Kay, whom he thinks to be dying, all the Romans and their allies are to be slaughtered. Afterward, Arthur buries his dead, and Kay and Bedivere recover. Arthur then sends the bodies of the Romans home as his "tribute." If this tribute is insufficient, he will give more of the same when he comes to Rome, he says.

Now Arthur moves southward, recapturing the lands taken by the Romans. While laying siege to a city in Tuscany, he sends Sir Florens, Gawain, and two other knights on a foraging expedition, with supportive forces. While the others graze their horses in a meadow, Gawain rides out to scout the countryside and meets a Saracen knight, with whom he fights. Each severely wounds the other before the Saracen submits. He tells Gawain that his name is Priamus and that because of his excessive pride his father sent him to this battle to humble him. When he asks Gawain's name, Gawain at first claims he is a mere yeoman, then admits the truth, and Priamus is thankful that he has lost to a man so worthy.

They return to the meadow where the horses are feeding, and Priamus heals both their wounds with the water of Paradise. Then Arthur's knights prepare for battle with the enemy force Priamus says is close at hand. The fight takes place, Priamus and his men join Arthur's side, and Arthur's men win. Back at the city walls, Arthur christens Priamus and makes him one of his own vassals. The siege on the city is successful, and Arthur promises mercy to all but the recreant duke. He orders his men not to molest the city's women.

Then Arthur moves on to be crowned in Rome, distributes land and wealth, and at last, at the request of his nobles — they have been too long parted from their wives, they say — he turns back toward England, where Guinevere and the other wives joyfully welcome him and all his troops.

Commentary

In "Arthur and King Lucius" Malory has transformed the alliterative *Morte Arthure,* one of the earliest full-scale tragedies in English, into a tale of the Round Table at its happiest and, in some ways, most noble. For the overweening pride of the Arthur in his source, Malory substitutes a just and wise king; and the poem's tragic conclusion, Arthur's return to fight Mordred, lover to Guinevere, Malory drops for a joyful reunion of faithful husbands and wives. In the source, Launcelot is a minor figure,

Gawain central. Malory elevates Launcelot, retains the dignity of Gawain, making only this distinction between them: Gawain's rash action in murdering Gaius is left unjustified, while the action of Launcelot and Cador on the road to Paris, labeled as rash in the source, is carefully rationalized here.

But the most important change is Malory's introduction of the marriage theme. The giant of St. Michael's Mountain wants Arthur's beard in the source. In Malory we are told twice that he wants Guinevere. The murdered duchess in this episode is changed from a cousin of Arthur to the *wife* of a cousin. And so, throughout Malory's version, all references to marriage in the source are retained and new references are introduced. At the same time, other love relationships are introduced and developed here. It is in this tale that we first see Gawain and Launcelot as devoted friends, fighting in one another's behalf. Arthur's love for Kay, present in the source, is retained and made central.

On another level, true kingship is obliquely identified with marital love, false kingship with rape. (It is a medieval commonplace that the relationship of the king and the state is "marriage.") The St. Michael's giant, as we have said, is emphatically identified with the rape of wives (the duchess; Guinevere).

In the source, Lucius' army includes Genoan giants; but Malory sets them in sharper relief by suppressing details which distract attention from the giants. Lucius' destruction of fair lands involves the murder of women and children (cf. the St. Michael's giant), while Arthur's capture of the Tuscan city, here as in the source, rules out harm to women, children, or anyone else other than the duke. The bear in Arthur's dream refers simultaneously (as in the source) to the tyrant Lucius and to the giant on the mountain. One further change Malory made was his introduction of parallels between Arthur and Henry V. (For discussion of this point, see Vinaver, *Works*, III, 1361-62.)

III. SIR LAUNCELOT DU LAKE

Launcelot du Lake returns from Rome most honored of all Arthur's knights and therefore most prized by the queen. He decides to seek knightly adventures, presumably to win still greater renown. He rides out with his nephew Sir Lionel and in the heat of noon goes to sleep under an apple tree. Lionel, keeping watch, sees a powerful knight overwhelm and tie up three weaker knights. When Lionel tries to help them he too is bound and carried back to the castle of the wicked Tarquin, where all four captives are stripped naked, beaten with thorns, and thrown into a dungeon. Ector, who has followed Launcelot and Lionel, is also caught.

While Launcelot is asleep under the tree, Morgan le Fay and three other ladies find him and fall in love with him. Morgan returns him to her castle by enchantment, and there the four ladies demand that he choose one of them or die. Launcelot refuses to choose any lady, and is saved by a maiden in return for his promise to help her father, Sir Bagdemagus, in his tournament.

Launcelot rides through a forest, finds a pavilion, and lies down to rest. A knight comes, mistakes his sleeping form for that of his lady, and lies down beside him. They fight, and Launcelot wounds the knight. The expected lady arrives and asks Launcelot to use his influence to make her knight one of the Round Table. Launcelot agrees.

The next morning he goes to the abbey where he is to meet Sir Bagdemagus. He wins the tournament for Sir Bagdemagus, then leaves to hunt for his nephew.

A damsel guides him to Tarquin, asking that if he wins this fight that he come to the aid of maidens distressed by a knight in the forest. While Launcelot and Tarquin fight, Tarquin explains that he persecutes knights because he is after the slayer of his brother—Launcelot. Sir Launcelot kills him, releases

Tarquin's latest prisoner, Sir Gaheris, and sends him to free the other prisoners; then Launcelot rides on. All the freed prisoners ride back to Camelot except Lionel, Ector, and Kay, who resolve to find Launcelot instead.

Launcelot, meanwhile, rides with the damsel, traps the thief and rapist who has been troubling maidens and kills him. As the damsel parts from him she advises him to marry, but Launcelot explains that neither marriage nor love of a mistress is fitting for a knight, for one ties him down and the other can involve him in wrong causes.

In time he comes to Tentagil Castle, where Uther conceived Arthur on Lady Igrayne—a castle where maidens have been imprisoned by giants for seven years. He slays the giants and rides on. He sleeps wherever he can and eventually comes to a castle where he is well lodged. That night he sees three knights attack a fourth—Sir Kay—and he leaps to Kay's rescue. Afterward, while Kay sleeps, Launcelot takes Kay's shield and armor, leaving his own, and rides off. In Launcelot's armor, Kay can ride home in peace, since no one will come against Launcelot. Launcelot, in the armor of boastful and unpopular Kay, has fights on his hands. He overcomes and impishly teases Ector, Ywain, and Gawain, among others, unhorsing them and leaving them so that they have "much sorow to gete their horsis agayne."

Following a hunting dog through the forest, Launcelot comes to a dead knight and his grieving lady. He consoles the lady, then departs and soon meets a damsel who tells him that the other knight in the recent battle, the damsel's brother, cannot be healed until some knight can be found who will go into the Chapel Perilous, find there a sword and bloody cloth, and bring them back to clean the wound. Launcelot goes, meets giant knights dressed in black who mysteriously make way for him when he charges; he takes the cloth and sword, and by perfect loyalty manages to escape the elaborate trap which has been set for him. Had he proved unfaithful either to the knightly code or to his virtuous love for the queen, he would have died, and the sorceress who loves him would have embalmed him to keep him at her side. He heals the wounded knight.

On the road again, he comes to a lady who asks that he retrieve her falcon from an elm tree, for if the hawk gets away her lord will kill her. Launcelot takes off his armor and gets the hawk. While he is up there, naked and unarmed, the lady's husband appears; the falcon was a trick, and the husband is here to murder him. Launcelot breaks off a branch, fights with that, and kills his would-be assassin. Next Launcelot encounters a knight who is about to kill his wife from jealousy. Though Launcelot tries to prevent the murder, the husband succeeds. Launcelot sends him to Camelot, where Guinevere imposes his penance and sends him for further penance to the pope.

At the feast of Pentecost, all Launcelot's great deeds are made known and he is acknowledged the greatest knight in the world.

Commentary

Whereas "Arthur and King Lucius" celebrates the chivalric ideal as it informs and supports the group, the tale of Launcelot celebrates the ideal as embodied in one man. Launcelot's encounter with Tarquin is an obvious contrast between the best of knights and one of the worst: Tarquin fights for personal vengeance and delight in cruelty, scorning the Order of Knighthood and all its laws; Launcelot fights in defense of the Order.

But from this point on, the tale is paradoxical. Forcing men to submit to Kay, then wearing Kay's armor, Launcelot seems to fight not for personal glory but for virtue's sake — the glory going, at least for the moment, to Kay. At the Chapel Perilous he proves his faithfulness; in other battles he proves his wit, his pluck, and his mercy. On the surface Launcelot's love of Guinevere is not a central concern in this tale; but one notices that while various characters speak of the rumor of Launcelot's love for Guinevere, Launcelot himself never admits to it. He in fact denies that he is in a position to love or that Guinevere is anything but faithful to Arthur.

Launcelot's expressed views on love and marriage contrast dramatically with those of Uther and the Arthur of the first tale, ironically recalled in this tale when Launcelot stumbles onto Tentagil Castle. When Launcelot hears that this is the castle where Arthur was adulterously conceived, Malory says cryptically, " 'Well,' seyde sir Launcelot, 'I understonde to whom this castel longith.' And so he departed frome them and betaught hem unto God." (The Tentagil episode is not found in Malory's sources.)

The reason Launcelot is Guinevere's knight at the end of the tale is that he is "the best in the world": her judgment of him is, as always, the judgment of civilization. Within this tale it is not shown that Launcelot has been seeking from her anything more than this symbolic approval. Nevertheless, Launcelot's behavior, even his language, as well as his attention to Guinevere, is nobler – more polite – than that of Arthur himself.

Malory does not develop the ironic and dangerous potential in all this; but the potential is clearly there. Malory alters his sources to make Launcelot send his prisoners to the queen rather than to Arthur, and he makes it clear that Launcelot's disguise as Kay actually fools no one. In the end, Kay has been made a fool of, and Launcelot has replaced him in Arthur's favor as well as the queen's.

In short, what appears on the surface to be an illustration of model knighthood is in fact, as Professor R. M. Lumiansky says, "a prelude to adultery," a central cause of the Round Table's fall. The final irony, which comes out more and more clearly as Le Morte Darthur progresses, is that it is chiefly Launcelot's need to prove himself to the lady he loves that makes him the great knight he is.

IV. THE TALE OF SIR GARETH

On the day of the Pentecost feast, when all the Round Table is assembled and Arthur, according to his custom, is waiting for some marvel to be revealed before he begins his meal, Sir Gawain announces the arrival of three men and a dwarf. One of the men, who at first seems unable to walk, then proves perfectly whole and agile, is "the goodlyest yonge man and the fayreste" the court has ever seen. He asks three gifts. For now he will name only the first: food and drink for a year.

Sir Kay scorns the young man as a "vylayne borne," on the grounds that "as he is, so he hath asked," and he mockingly calls him "Beaumains," that is, "pretty hands." Kay says he'll make the boy work in the kitchen. Gawain and Launcelot defend the boy, but Kay is obstinate and the boy goes with him willingly. Gawain had reason to be kind to Beaumains, Malory says, "for that proffer com of his bloode, for he was nere kyn to hym than he wyste of"; Launcelot's kindness, on the other hand, "was of his grete jantylnesse and curtesy."

The following Pentecost, a damsel named Lynet arrives at court to ask help for her sister, whose castle is under siege by the Red Knight of the Red Lands. She will not tell her sister's name, so Arthur refuses to send any of his knights with her. Now Beaumains asks the remaining two gifts: that he be assigned this adventure and that he be knighted by Launcelot. Arthur agrees.

Lynet is furious when she sees a kitchen boy assigned to her, but she has no choice. Beaumains' dwarf produces a splendidly dressed horse and fine armor, to all the court's amazement, and Beaumains rides off without spear or shield. Kay follows to mock him and Beaumains takes Kay's spear and shield. Beamains tells Launcelot, who has seen all this, that he is Gawain's brother Gareth.

He is knighted and, bearing Kay's shield (cf. Launcelot in the preceding tale), begins a series of adventures each more difficult than the last, throughout which Lynet belittles and scorns him. He beats six thieves, two knights at a bridge, the Black Knight, the Green Knight, Sir Persaunt of Inde, and at last the Red Knight of the Red Lands. Lynet finally comes to approve him.

Now Lyonesse requires that he serve her faithfully for a year in order to win her love. He does so, and in further encounters proves his might, pluck, and chastity. He and Lyonesse plan a tournament at which Gareth is to win her as his lady. After the tournament, but before Gareth rejoins Lyonesse, he fights the Brown Knight without Pity (Bereuse Saunz Pité) and—unknowingly—his own brother Gawain. Lyonesse stops the final battle by making the two brothers known to each other; then Gareth and Lyonesse are married at Arthur's court.

Commentary

The tale of Gareth, besides being long, is one of the most complex in all *Le Morte Darthur,* both in plot and in its organization of textural and structural details. It will be possible here to suggest only its general place in the total tragedy. The tale brings together themes from the two preceding tales, "Arthur and King Lucius," and "Launcelot du Lake." As Lancelot kills Tarquin, so Gareth kills Bereuse. As Launcelot wears Kay's shield and armor, thus *appearing* to work for virtue's sake, not for personal glory, Gareth, using the same shield, does indeed work for virtue's sake—only Kay and Launcelot ever know of the shield.

His humble entry as a seeming cripple, his year in the kitchen, his meek toleration of Lynet's abuse, and his year of service to Lyonesse all suggest his humility. More perfectly than any other knight, Gareth lives by both the letter and the spirit of the Pentecostal oath established by Arthur at the end of "Tor and Pellanor." He is the embodiment of mercy, renouncing even the avenging justice—blood payment—most closely associated throughout the *Morte Darthur* with his brother Gawain. For all his love of Gawain, Gareth will not defend murder or vengeance even when Gawain is guilty of them. Seeing that Gawain is "evir vengeable," Gareth shuns him, seeking out Launcelot instead.

Gareth is also the ideal lover, contrasting with both his close friends, Launcelot and Tristram, whose love, for all its virtuous loyalty, is adulterous. The true end of love, Gareth's story shows,

44

is marriage. And all the symbolic extensions of the ideal of marriage which Malory had earlier set up in "Arthur and King Lucius" are reintroduced here.

Gareth's tale ends in his own marriage and that of his brothers, followed by the related ritual of feudal commendation, wherein all those who have been overcome or rescued by Gareth come to pledge their fealty in return for his protection as overlord; the ending then widens out to Arthur's parallel dispersing of titles and lands.

In the tale of Gareth, Malory presents the high point in the rise and fall of Arthur's kingdom. Almost every motif here has its analog in "Arthur and King Lucius," but whereas that tale concerns a noble kingdom at war, Gareth's tale concerns a kingdom in time of peace. Every element in the tale reflects the elegance, the ritualistic pomp and circumstance of a peacetime kingdom: the knights Gareth fights are all identified with clear, bold colors—black, green, red, india-blue, red again, and brown—and great tournaments formally divide the main action. It should be added, incidentally, that the tale (Malory's clearest departure from any known source) introduces one of his most brilliant creations of character—the sharp-tongued Lynet.

V. SIR TRISTRAM DE LYONES*

1. Isode the Fair

In the days when Merlin was still free, King Melyodas de Lyones married the sister of King Mark of Cornwall and had a son by her, called Tristram, "the sorrowfull-borne." The circumstances of his birth are vaguely analogous to those attending the birth of Arthur: the death of a parent—in this case Tristram's mother—unrest in the kingdom, aid to the throne from Merlin. Seven years later King Melyodas marries again. His new wife, wishing that her own sons might succeed to the throne, plots to kill Tristram. When her plot is discovered she is sentenced to

*For commentary on the whole Tristram section, see p. 54.

burn, but Tristram himself pleads mercy for her and saves her. Melyodas sends Tristram to France, where he becomes a great huntsman and harper. At eighteen he returns to his father's hall.

Tristram distinguishes himself by killing Marhault and thus freeing King Mark of a debt of tribute owed to King Angwyssh of Ireland; but after the fight Tristram has wounds that cannot be healed except back in Ireland, where he got them. He returns, taking his harp, and is soon called to Angwyssh's court to play. He goes, converting his name to Tramtrist, and says nothing of his fight with Marhault, the queen's brother. Angwyssh's daughter Isode heals Tristram and they fall in love. He defeats her suitor Sir Palomydes in a tournament and forces him to abandon his suit for the moment.

But now Tristram's identity is discovered. Reluctantly, King Angwyssh expels him from court; Tristram says farewell to Isode and returns to Mark at Tentagil Castle. He serves Mark for some time, but at last Tristram and Mark fall out over a lady, the wife of Sir Segwarydes. Mark tries to murder Tristram but fails. Soon afterward Tristram finds the lady not worth his love, as he thinks, and vows he will henceforth "beware what maner of lady I shall love or truste."

Mark, still plotting to murder Tristram, sends him after Isode, whom he intends to marry on the basis of Tristram's praise of her. Tristram's ship is driven to England in a storm, and there by chance King Angwyssh has been summoned to defend himself against an accusation of murder. Tristram offers himself as Angwyssh's champion in a trial by combat and fights Launcelot's cousin Blamoure. He beats him but refuses to kill him, and so Tristram both frees King Angwyssh and becomes a friend of Launcelot's house. King Angwyssh offers Tristram any gift he may ask, and Tristram requests Isode, not for himself but for Mark, as his mission requires.

Isode and Tristram sail for Mark's court in Cornwall. On the way, a love potion prepared for Isode and King Mark accidentally falls into the hands of Tristram and Isode, who unwittingly drink it and thus seal their unlucky love. Before reaching Cornwall Tristram has further adventures which by chance parallel adventures Launcelot is undergoing at the same time. Then the lovers arrive at court; Isode and Mark are married, but she and Tristram remain lovers.

Palomydes shows up and again Tristram fights him. Then all goes well for a time, until Andret, Tristram's cousin, jealous of Tristram's glory, shows King Mark that Tristram is talking with Isode at her window. (Cf. Launcelot's window visit with Guinevere much later.) Mark attacks, Tristram ludicrously overcomes and humiliates him—chasing the king and slapping him with the flat of his sword until the king falls on his nose. Afterward, Mark's advisers recommend that he make peace with Tristram, the best of his protectors, and Mark gloomily does so.

But Tristram's troubles are by no means over. Lamerok of Wales, partly to get revenge on Tristram for shaming him once, and partly to divert to Mark's court troubles that must otherwise come to Arthur's, sends King Mark a magical cup which can reveal whether women are loyal. When Isode fails the test, Mark's advisers tell him not to trust a mere sorcerer's cup.

Andret then lies in wait with twelve knights in Isode's bedroom and, when Tristram lies down naked beside her, leaps out and seizes him, binds him, and takes him to the king. Tristram reminds the court of all he had done for Cornwall, but Andret scoffs and prepares to kill him on the spot. Tristram breaks free, kills Andret, and escapes. After this Tristram and Isode live happily for a time in a forest hut, but at last Mark gets Isode back and imprisons her.

Tristram, again suffering a wound that will not heal—and now unable to get to Isode for help—is forced to go to Britain, to another lady, Isode le Blaunche Maynes. Time passes and at last Tristram marries the new Isode but will not consummate the marriage. He hears now that Launcelot scorns him for his falsehood to his lady. Guinevere meanwhile writes letters of comfort to La Beal Isode.

2. Lamerok of Wales
3. Sir La Cote Male Tale

Both Lamerok and Tristram happen to be shipwrecked on an island ruled by Nabon le Noire, a murderer of knights. The two write off their old differences and join against Nabon and overthrow him. Tristram returns to Britain afterward, while Lamerok fights with various knights, including Launcelot and Gawain, and proves himself.

The tale of Sir La Cote Male Tale concerns a third rising hero, one who defends Guinevere from a lion and is therefore knighted by Arthur. His coat is tattered with the sword strokes that murdered his father; Kay gives him, for this reason, the name "The Knight with the Ugly Coat."

The young man accepts a guest no one else will take and rides off with the damsel Maledysaunt ("Ugly-talking") who has brought it. Two established knights knock Male Tale from his saddle but choose not to fight with him on foot, and the damsel bitterly mocks her champion. He later fights a courtyard full of knights and slays twelve of them, but still the lady mocks him. When Mordred and Launcelot try to defend him, the lady turns her tongue against them as well.

At last, when the great Sir Launcelot scolds her, she weepingly explains that she mocks the boy only because she fears he will be harmed in this adventure. Launcelot changes her name to the Damsel Beau-Pensaunte (loosely, "beautiful of thought"). Launcelot and Male Tale purge Castle Pendragon of the four outlaw knights who rule and, and for his bravery the boy is promised a seat at the Round Table next Pentecost. At that time Male Tale marries Beau-Pensaunte.

4. Tristram's Madness and Exile
5. The Castle of Maidens

Tristram and Lamerok meet again by accident, this time in the Perilous Forest of North Wales. They unwittingly fight each other, then again swear friendship. They meet Palomydes, who unhorses them both and rides on in pursuit of his beast. Now Tristram and Lamerok part and undergo separate adventures, many of them involving single combat with Round Table knights.

Arthur is in the Perilous Forest through the craft of a sorceress, Aunowre, who captured him to make him her lover and, finding he will not be faithless to Guinevere, now hopes to destroy him by sending him, without his identifying arms, against all the knights who, to increase their glory, fight any who happen to pass. Arthur's knights, here to hunt for him, are unwittingly his most dangerous enemies.

Tristram meanwhile reaches Cornwall and Isode, discovers love letters that have passed between her and another knight, and goes mad. He runs naked for a time, then recovers and is exiled by Mark. In exile he encounters the Round Table knights who are looking for Arthur. He beats many of them, helps Launcelot when his life is threatened by Morgan le Fay, helps Gawain, and enters a tournament near the Castle of Maidens.

At the tournament he tells no one his name—fights under the title "The Knight with the Black Shield"—and on the first two days departs secretly after he has won the field. On the third day he beats and shames his old enemy Palomydes, fights Arthur himself to a standstill, then is wounded almost mortally by an accidental stroke from Launcelot. He flees to a forest; Palomydes follows him to kill him; but despite his wound Tristram beats Palomydes, then Gawain's brother Gaheris. Launcelot, still at the tournament, is declared winner of the field but gives the prize to Tristram as more deserving.

Ten of Arthur's best men go to find Tristram. Launcelot, riding in the wrong direction, rescues a damsel; Lucan and Ywain unwittingly fight with Tristram and are beaten. Tristram is finally found not by Arthur's men but by an enemy—the father of a man he killed in the tournament—and is thrown in prison along with Sir Dynadin and Palomydes. Tristram falls sick.

6. The Round Table

Gaheris and other Round Table knights visit King Mark's court and report Tristram's great deeds. While they are there a challenge comes to Mark's court from Ywain of the Round Table. None of Mark's knights can withstand him, and the visiting Round Table knights are sworn never knowingly to ride against a fellow Round Table knight except in sport. In idiotic fury, Mark himself attacks Ywain — from ambush. Kay scoffs at Mark's cowardice and rebukes him for sending his best knight, Sir Tristram, into exile. Spitefully Mark and Andret decide to way-lay Kay and Gaheris. They put on black clothes so that they won't be seen in the dark, forgetting that it is a bright moonlit night. Kay and Gaheris easily trounce them.

Meanwhile the jailor of Tristram, Palomydes, and Dynadin reconsiders and releases the knights from prison. Dynadin en-counters the murderer of knights, Bereuse Saunz Pité (whose later death at Gareth's hands has already been recounted), and puts him to flight. Tristram falls into Morgan's hands and is tricked into bearing for her a shield designed to embarrass Launcelot and Guinevere. He uses the shield in a tournament where he unhorses both Arthur and Ywain.

Afterward, riding in a forest, Tristram finds Bereuse Saunz Pité about to murder Palomydes. He rescues his old enemy, drives off Bereuse, and sets a time and place for battle with Palomydes. They will fight beside the old tomb of Lanceor (see "The Knight with the Two Swords"). As they ride on they find a strange knight with a covered shield sleeping under a tree. They wake him; he mounts his horse and jousts them both to the ground, then gallops off. Tristram finds later that the stranger has slain another Round Table knight, has wounded Gawain and Bleoberys, and has shamed Kay and Dynadin.

Tristram rides to the appointed place for his fight with Palomydes — the tomb of Lanceor, where long ago Merlin prophesied that the two greatest knights and the two greatest friends in the world would fight. There he finds the knight with the covered shield and fights him. At last, both badly wounded, Tristram and Launcelot discover one another's identity and the fight stops. They go to Camelot, where Launcelot explains that, riding incognito, he was forced into battle with Round Table knights. Tristram is made a knight of the Round Table and all the court rejoices.

7. King Mark

King Mark, jealous as ever, and disgusted by the incessant talk of Tristram's virtues, decides to capture and murder Tristram. His men refuse the plot, and when he murders one, the rest say they will go to Arthur and declare him a traitor. Mark says he will go himself and rides away. He meets Sir Lamerok and Sir Dynadin, fights them and loses miserably, then rides with them, not revealing his name. At Tor's castle Mark is found out, and Dynadin, much as Mark disgusts him, decides to conduct him on the way to Arthur. They meet a group of Round Table knights and Mark flees.

Led by Arthur's fool, the Round Table knights trick and mock King Mark and chase him through the forest hooting and howling until Mark has the luck to stumble onto Sir Palomydes, who protects him. Mark rides with his protector until Palomydes abandons him in disgust. Alone again, Palomydes stands in the forest bemoaning his hopeless love of Isode, and both Mark and Dynadin overhear him. Mark sneaks away and, for lack of anywhere else to go, goes to Camelot to suffer Arthur's judgment. He jousts with Amante and by a cowardly stroke kills him, then flees. Launcelot brings him back, for love of Tristram, and Mark swears on the Bible that he will now be Tristram's faithful lord — a lie, of course. Meanwhile Palomydes fights Lamerok, neither knowing who the other is, then the two ride separately to the tournament Arthur has announced at Camelot.

At the tournament, Gawain wins the first day's prize. On the second he and his brothers are overthrown by Lamerok and swear vengeance. The enmity between Gawain's brothers and

Lamerok is an old one. "And wyte you well, my fayre bretherne," Gawain says, "that this sir Lameroke woll nevyr love us, because we slew his fadir, kynge Pellynor, for we demed that he slew oure fadir, kynge Lotte of Orkenay; and for the deth of kynge Pellynor sir Lameroke ded us a shame to oure modir. Therefore I woll be revenged."

Soon after the tournament, Lamerok goes to the lady he has loved and served, Lot's widow, Gawain's mother. Gaheris comes into the bedroom, kills his mother, and says he will kill Lamerok if they meet when Lamerok is armed. Gawain's brothers Mordred and Aggravain fight Dynadin because of his friendship with Lamerok.

Meanwhile King Mark, safe in Cornwall, writes a scornful letter to Arthur and another to Guinevere accusing her of faithlessness. Mark's enemies invade his land and, little as he likes it, he is forced to ask Tristram's help. Tristram deploys Mark's forces, fights nobly himself, and wins Cornwall's battle. Afterward a song mocking King Mark is sung at Mark's court—a song composed by Dynadin. Mark is sure Tristram had a hand in this, but he can do nothing.

8. Alexander the Orphan

After Tristram's defeat of the men of Sessoynes, Mark's brother Bodwyne defeats a great army of Saracens. Jealous of Bodwyne's valor, Mark murders him and tries to murder his wife and child as well. The child, Alexander, escapes and grows up in a distant country. (Cf. Tristram.) When he is old enough to be knighted he goes after King Mark, but he is sidetracked first by Morgan, then by love and the game of challenging knights for the increase of his own glory. Mark gets the chance to strike first and murders him.

9. The Tournament at Surluse

Galahalt, lord of Surluse, holds a seven-day tournament, and many of Arthur's knights enlist, some of them in disguise. The tournament comes off splendidly, or so it appears: glorious fighting, feasting, plenty of romance. But the joy of the tournament is not perfect. With every honor won by Pellanor's sons, Gawain and his brothers grow more jealous and more firmly committed to getting their revenge. Moreover, the purpose of the tournament is not as innocent as it seems. It has been set up by Galahalt and the Haute Prince to murder Sir Launcelot, whose glory they envy.

10. Joyous Gard

Knowing that the tournament at Surluse has been set up as a way of killing Launcelot, Mark sends Tristram in hopes that he will be mistaken for the disguised Launcelot. Tristram is hurt but not killed, and Mark, offering to dress his wounds himself, gets Tristram alone and throws him in a dungeon. Percival of Wales rescues him; Launcelot gives Tristram and Isode his own castle, Joyous Gard; and Mark is thrown in prison by his own vassals. While at Joyous Gard, Tristram goes hunting every day, taking arms with him at Isode's request. He meets Palomydes, Ector, Bereuse Saunz Pité, and others.

Word comes that Lamerok has been murdered by Gawain and Gaheris, and when Tristram meets them he spares them only for love of Arthur. He later meets Gareth, Gawain's nobler brother, and finds him repelled by the treachery of his brothers. Later Tristram and his companions come upon a barge carrying the murdered king of the Red City, in whose dead hand lies a letter asking for vengeance. Palomydes takes the quest and departs. Tristram and the rest have adventures of their own. Throughout this tale Sir Dynadin scoffs at lovers and repeatedly gets buffeted by mistake because of other people's love affairs and jealousies.

11. The Red City

Palomydes avenges the death of the king of the Red City and then, riding with Tristram and Sir Dynadin again, meets Bereuse Saunz Pité, whom he fails to recognize and allows to escape. The three prepare then to leave for Arthur's tournament at Lonezep.

12. The Tournament at Lonezep

Tristram, Palomydes, Gareth, and their followers decide to joust against King Arthur's side, since they can win more honor by overcoming Arthur's knights than by supporting them. Palomydes fights better than ever before because Isode is watching. On the second day, warned by Dynadin and Gareth of Palomydes' envy, Tristram prevents Palomydes from winning more honor. On the third day Launcelot wins the prize, and Palomydes finally reveals the full measure of his envy.

13. Sir Palomydes

Palomydes is captured and condemned to die for killing a lord in fair fight at the tournament at Lonezep (cf. "Tristram's Madness and Exile"). He is rescued by Launcelot backed up by Tristram and borne to Joyous Gard. While Palomydes is there Tristram learns that Palomydes has never renounced his old love for Isode. Tristram again challenges him to a fight. Three days before the appointed time, Tristram is accidentally wounded by an archer (cf. "Sir Launcelot and Queen Guinevere," Part 3), so that he cannot meet Palomydes. Palomydes rides off greatly relieved, and Tristram, as soon as he is well, begins to hunt him.

14. Launcelot and Elayne

Riding in search of adventure, Launcelot comes upon a castle where a beautiful lady has been under a curse for five years. He kills a dragon, meets Pellas, son of the Maimed King, and sees the Grail. By a trick, Launcelot is made to lie with Pellas' daughter Elayne, and that night Galahad is conceived. After Launcelot leaves, Sir Bors comes to the castle. He sees visions and hears that though Launcelot is the best of worldly knights, many shall surpass him in spiritual things.

Soon after, Arthur has a feast for his knights, and Lady Elayne comes to it. Launcelot is again tricked into lying with her. Guinevere discovers it and banishes him. Launcelot leaps out a window and runs mad from grief. Arthur's knights ride off to hunt for him and have various adventures, including some involving the Grail.

Launcelot meanwhile goes from place to place until the Lady Elayne recognizes him and, through her father, arranges for his healing by the Grail. Believing he is still banished from England, Launcelot asks lodgings from Pellas. He is given a castle, which he names The Joyous Isle, and there he lives under a false name, with Elayne as his servant. In this castle Percival and Ector eventually find him. They return with him to Arthur's hall just in time for the feast of Pentecost, and all the court rejoices at his return.

Conclusion

Tristram, too, prepares to go to the Pentecost feast. Isode refuses to go because her appearance as his lady would make men challenge him to fights. Tristram must not stay away though, she says, because his station requires him to go. Tristram goes and on the way meets his old enemy Palomydes. They fight, then for the last time drop their quarrel and vow to be friends henceforth. Palomydes, having now fulfilled an old vow involving seven great battles, agrees to be christened.

Commentary

The Tristram section of *Le Morte Darthur* takes up nearly a third of the total work and seems from a modern point of view an enormous digression: Arthur's knights figure in the Tristram story, but centrally the plot concerns not Arthur's court but that of a petty vassal to Arthur, King Mark. To the medieval reader, with his different but no less sophisticated esthetic expectations, the Tristram section would seem not a digression but a parallel, a second story juxtaposed with the first to serve as an exploration of the first story's meaning. The Tristram story rings changes on the whole Arthur story; that is, it presents every possible variation on the themes set up in the Arthur story, with the ultimate purpose of demonstrating dramatically that, whatever the particulars may be, once one has entered the trap of glory and chivalry, there is no way out.

Tristram's story in some ways recalls Arthur's: born while his father is presumed dead, Tristram is nearly slain by servants who would like to rule the barony themselves (cf. Lot, etc.); he is aided by Merlin and raised by foster parents; one of his first accomplishments is to overthrow a claim for tribute (cf. Arthur and Lucius); and as Arthur kills a giant who has murdered the wife of his cousin, Tristram kills a giant who has murdered his cousin.

In other respects Tristram's story parallels that of Launcelot (part of whose story has not yet appeared in Malory's legend): both run mad from love-despair; each loves the queen of his respective lord; both are trapped in bed by knights jealous of their personal glory; both are driven out of court when their adultery is proved; both plead (in identical phrases) for pardon because of their long service to the state; each triggers civil war but later becomes crucial to his lord's defense of his kingdom against enemies: Tristram, pardoned by Mark, saves Cornwall, while Launcelot, not pardoned until too late, cannot move his forces to England in time to save it.

There are countless parallels of this kind, not only in the main plots but in even the most trivial incidents involving minor characters. The story of La Cote Male Tale, who ends up happily married, closely parallels Gareth's story—but with grim complications introduced by the fact that nearly everyone he meets is in disguise. Lamerok's love for King Lot's widow (Gawain's mother) and Palomydes' love for Tristram's mistress (King Mark's wife, Isode) ironically comment on the love stories of Tristram and Launcelot. Lamerok's love, which shames the lady, intensifies the Lamerok-Gawain feud. Palomydes' futile love for Isode, like Tristram's love for the same lady and like Launcelot's love for Guinevere, makes the lover a valorous fighting man but also involves him in wrong causes.

Mark's story, too, comments on the Arthur story. King Mark is stupid, cowardly, and thoroughly vicious; but though he is comically incapable of winning any glory on his own, he is driven by the same motive as any bold knight: desire for glory greater than any other man's. He may not kill those who stand above him by honest battle, but he manages to get rid of them, or some of them. (Eventually he even manages to bungle through a successful murder of Sir Tristram.)

One of the central symbols organizing these parallels is the idea of disguise. Every knight rides in disguise at one time or another in the Tristram section, and the apparent reason is that the chivalric system is overripe. The great knights who won their legitimate glory in war against the infidel, in defense of the kingdom, or in defense of the innocent—such men as Launcelot, Gawain, and Lamerok—are now too well known and too much feared to add to their glory (as they must do to hold their ladies' interest) in the old way. Since all men now fear them, they no longer change their shields as a sign (or even pretense) of humility; they change them in order to dupe poor fools into fighting. Cowardly knights, on the other hand, change their shields to escape the vengeance of the relatives of those they have murdered or killed in more or less legitimate battle. Thus great knights, disguised, slaughter or maim one another in the challenge game or defending the innocence of their far from innocent ladies, while wicked knights, also disguised, prey on the weakened and on strays.

Superficially this insanity seems glorious, a colossal sort of football, and Sir Dynadin's voice of common sense seems ludicrous. Riding with Tristram, Dynadin curses the day he fell into the company of this battle-happy fool who can never pass a knight without trying him or circle a castle where knights insist on challenging all who pass by. When Isode flirtatiously asks Dynadin how he can ever become a great knight if he won't fight for the love of some lady, Sir Dynadin's answer is comically blunt: "'God deffende me!' seyde sir Dynadan, 'for the joy of love is to shorte, and the sorow thereof and what cometh thereof is duras over longe.'" And when Isode goes further, teasingly asking if he will fight for her against three cruel knights, Dyna-din replies: "I shall sey you ye be as fayre a lady as evir I sawe ony, and much fayrer than is my lady quene Gwenyver, but wyte you well, at one worde, I woll nat fyght for you wyth three knyghtes, Jesu me defende!" He is comic because he won't play by the rules; but as the rest of the *Morte Darthur* makes clear, he is right.

The Tristram section does directly develop one important strand of the Arthur story. The Lamerok-Gawain feud is intensi-fied, and allegiances on each side are made firm through tour-naments and encounters in the challenge game. When Gawain and his brothers learn that Pellanor was *not* the murderer of their father—they only "demed" he was—they have already gone too far to back down. Appearance has become reality; the disguise has become the man.

VI. THE TALE OF THE HOLY GRAIL*

1. The Departure

At the feast of Pentecost a damsel comes and asks that Sir Launcelot come with her. He goes and meets Galahad, his son, makes him a knight, and invites him to court. Launcelot rides to court ahead. Magic writing appears on the Sege Perilous—the seat at the Round Table which no man has yet been worthy enough to fill—revealing that the seat will be filled today.

Then Arthur and his court hear of a sword in a floating stone, and on the pommel a legend claiming that this sword belongs to the best knight in the world. The king suggests that the sword belongs to Launcelot, but Launcelot says no and refuses to try to draw it out. The sword has a curse, he says: the man who tries to pull it out and fails will get a grievous wound from it later. Arthur orders Gawain to try and he does so willingly, accepting the curse because it was at Arthur's command. Then Percival tries it "to beare sir Gawayne felyship" in the curse. Galahad arrives, takes the Sege Perilous, and acquires the sword.

*For commentary on the whole Grail section, see p. 66.

Then the Grail Quest begins. Because he knows he will never see all his knights together again, Arthur orders a tournament at Camelot. Galahad, riding without any shield, proves himself brilliantly. At the feast afterward, the Grail appears, hidden under drapes, and feeds all the hall. Most of Arthur's knights vow to go on the Grail Quest, and to the sorrow of Arthur and his queen, they depart.

2. The Miracles

After Sir Bagdemagus fails, Galahad wins a miraculous white shield marked with a red cross. The white knight who defends the shield tells Galahad its history — it comes from the days of Joseph of Aramathy and has healing powers — then the white knight vanishes. Galahad's squire, who has heard all this, asks that he may follow wherever Galahad goes. When Galahad hints that he must ride alone, the squire asks to be knighted. Galahad grants it.

Now Galahad is directed to a churchyard where a ghost howls, weakening men and driving them mad. Galahad lifts the lid of the haunted coffin, drives out a fiend, and orders the body removed from holy ground. A good man explains the allegory in the event: the body signifies the foulness of the world, corrupt with the hatred of fathers and sons — one of the reasons Christ was born of a Virgin.

Galahad and his former squire, now Sir Melias, ride together until the road forks. A magic sign says that the left fork can lead to proof of prowess, the right to proof of knightly bearing and personal virtue as well. Melias takes the left. He finds a crown on a throne in a meadow and takes it with him. A knight comes against him and nearly kills him. Galahad arrives to beat the knight and also a second knight, then takes Melias back to an abbey, where he is eventually healed. Galahad learns that in taking the left fork — the road to prowess — Melias acted with pride; in taking the crown he acted with covetousness. The two knights Galahad overcame signify Galahad's triumph over these two sins. No man with such sins in him can achieve the Grail Quest.

Soon after, while Galahad is praying in a chapel, a voice sends him to break the cruel customs of the Maidens' Castle, and he goes. For seven years the castle has been held by seven brothers who murder knights and constrain maidens. Galahad drives the brothers off (he never kills except when God wishes), and Sir Gawain, Sir Gareth, and Sir Ywain slay them. The castle, it turns out, signifies the good souls imprisoned before the Incarnation; the seven knights are the deadly sins; and Galahad is a figure of Christ. Galahad was right, Gawain learns, to let the seven flee. He and his companions are wrong in needlessly murdering. Gawain accepts this but refuses any penance, believing the pains he suffers in battle are penance enough.

Galahad, meanwhile, encounters Launcelot and Percival, who do not know him because he is disguised. He unhorses them both, and when a hermit reveals his identity he rides away from them and out of sight. Launcelot, leaving Percival to seek adventures on his own, comes to a mysterious chapel and soon falls asleep on his shield at the gate. Half-sleeping, half-waking, he sees a sick knight healed by the Grail. Launcelot tries to come fully awake but cannot stir.

The healed knight takes Launcelot's horse, helmet, and sword, and after he is gone a voice tells Launcelot he is harder than stone, more bitter than wood, and more naked than the leaf of the fig tree. He walks to a hermitage and learns what all this means. He has won renown for love of Guinevere, not for love of God; he has fought for right and wrong with equal spirit and all for personal glory or love. The time has come when he must recognize God's kingship whether he likes it or not. Launcelot laments his sins and prays that he may become a better man.

3. Sir Percival

With the object of finding Galahad and overcoming him for his own greater glory, Percival asks an old recluse about

Galahad's whereabouts. The recluse, Percival's aunt, tells him that his mother is dead from sorrow at his abandoning her for the fellowship of the Round Table and that the Round Table was created by Merlin as a symbol of the World, a place of false security which can lead to overweening pride. By Merlin's prophecy, only three Round Table Knights shall achieve the Grail Quest—two virgin knights and one who is chaste; and the best of these is Galahad.

Percival repents his proud wish to beat Galahad for glory, and his aunt tells him the way. Riding on, he comes upon a wounded knight four hundred years old, Sir Evelake, or Mordrayns, who in the days of Joseph of Aramathy, asked God that he not be allowed to die until he had seen the knight who would achieve the Grail Quest. The Lord granted Evelake's wish and promised that when Sir Evelake saw the Grail knight he would at last be healed.

Percival goes to find Galahad for him but is attacked by twenty knights who manage to kill his horse before Galahad saves Percival's life. Galahad then rides away again, still insisting on pursuing the quest alone. Percival walks in the forest, gets the gift of a hackney from a distressed squire, meets with a man on a black horse who kills the hackney and scornfully rides off.

Then a lady appears and gives him a black horse in return for his service. The horse runs four days' journey in an hour and is about to plunge into the sea when Percival crosses himself in fright and breaks the horse's demonic power. It shakes him off and goes flaming and howling into the water. Now Percival sees a serpent fighting a lion. He takes the lion's part, because it is a nobler beast, and kills the serpent. In a dream, the lady who owns the lion praises him and the lady of the serpent demands that, in payment for her pet, he become her man. He refuses.

A holy man comes to him on a white ship and explains the allegory: the lady of the lion is the New Law—faith, hope, belief, and baptism; the lady of the serpent is the Old Law, served by fiends (the black horse and serpent), and her request that he be her man was a temptation.

The holy man departs, and now a black ship comes. A beautiful maiden tells Percival lies, gets him drunk, and lies naked with him in a splendid pavilion. Percival crosses himself; pavilion and lady vanish. The holy man returns, explains that the lady was the Devil himself, and that henceforth he must be more careful. The holy man vanishes and Percival boards his ship and leaves the place.

4. Sir Launcelot

Launcelot and an old holy man see a devil sitting over a corpse in a splendid shirt. The devil tells them the dead man was a good man who was killed in a fire which did not singe a hair on his body. He is now in heaven. Then the devil leaves and they bury the corpse. The holy man tells Launcelot to take some of the dead man's hair and put it next to his skin, and to eat no meat and drink no wine if he hopes to have any success. Launcelot obeys and rides on.

He meets a lady on a white palfrey who tells him he has in the past been closer than he is now to the adventure he seeks, then tells him he will find good lodging tomorrow but not tonight. That night, sleeping in the forest, Launcelot dreams that God comes down and blesses nine knights but rebukes one of them as having wasted himself on worldliness. From a hermit Launcelot learns that the first seven knights are his ancestors, the sinful eighth knight is himself, and the ninth, Galahad.

Riding on, Launcelot comes to a castle and a tournament of black knights against white. He joins the black because they are weaker, so that helping them to victory will mean greater honor for Launcelot; but he is driven out by the knights in white. He rests under an apple tree, where an old man comes to him in his sleep and reproaches him as evil, faithless, and full of sin.

An old woman explains the symbolism of the tournament: among those knights of Arthur's court who took on themselves the Grail Quest, some were pure, some sinful, and the sinful will fail. In joining the black knights from vainglory, Launcelot chose the side suitable to him.

That night Launcelot encounters the man on the black horse, who attacks and slays Launcelot's horse just as he earlier slew Percival's.

5. Sir Gawain

Sir Gawain rides for a long time without any adventures. He meets Sir Ector and learns that most of the knights have been having similar bad luck; there is no word of Galahad, Launcelot, Percival, or Bors. Ector and Gawain come to an abandoned chapel, where they fall asleep. Gawain has a vision of a fair meadow, a hayrack, two white bulls and one white except for a black spot, and many black bulls which leave the meadow and grow lean. The three white bulls are tied by ropes. Sir Ector dreams that he and Launcelot leap from a chair onto two horses; Launcelot falls from his horse and then, clothed in a knotted coat and riding on an ass, stops at a well to drink from it, but the water sinks away from him. Ector rides on and comes to a rich man's house where there is a wedding, but he is turned away.

Then, awakening, Ector and Gawain see a hand holding a bridle and bearing a candle into the chapel. A voice calls them knights full of "evil faith and poor belief" and tells them "these two things" have failed them. They go to find a hermit who can interpret these signs and on the way encounter a knight who offers battle. Gawain fights and accidentally kills the man—a fellow Round Table knight, Sir Ywain. Ector and Gawain bury him, then go on to the hermit.

The hermit explains that the meadow of Gawain's dream represents the Round Table and also the virtues *humility* and *patience*, which are always green and vital. The black bulls represent proud and sinful knights; they grow lean—that is, their group is decimated—for lack of humility and patience. The white bulls are sinless knights whose humility is represented by the ropes. The sinful knights slay each other "and they that shall ascape shall be so megir that hit shall be marvayle to se them." As for the two pure white bulls—Galahad and Percival—and the spotted white bull—Bors—two of these will vanish and one will return.

In Ector's dream, the chair signifies the royal line from which both Ector and Launcelot are born; Launcelot's fall means that he has humbled himself; the knotted coat is his humiliation of the flesh; the ass represents his humility; the sinking well refers to God's grace, now withdrawn from him. He shall suffer twenty-four days at the hands of the Devil, one for each year of sin, then return to Camelot.

The hand with the bridle, seen by both Gawain and Ector, signifies the Holy Ghost where charity abides, and abstinence; the candle represents the way of Christ. Ector and Gawain, lacking charity, abstinence, and truth, will not achieve the Grail Quest. The cause of Gawain's lack of adventures is his character as murderer. The holy man says he would like to counsel Gawain, but Gawain has no time for that yet, he says, and hurries away to catch up with Sir Ector.

6. Sir Bors

Bors meets Launcelot and accepts his advice to eat only bread and water and to wear no proud knightly clothes but only a plain shirt under his armor. Riding on his way, Bors sees a bird which kills itself for its young. He comes to a castle where a lady asks him to fight as her champion; he agrees to do so, then goes to bed and dreams.

Bors sees a white bird which offers him riches, then a black bird which asks him to serve her tomorrow, for her blackness can do far more for him than the other's whiteness. In a second dream he sees a chapel with a chair in it, on the left of the chair a worm-eaten tree, on the right two lilies; the tree desires to take the life from the lilies but is prevented; then from these flowers come many more. A wise man says, "Guard yourself lest any such adventure befall you."

The next day Bors fights for the lady and wins without killing his enemy. As Bors rides on he finds his brother Sir Lionel naked and bound, being beaten with thorns. The same instant he sees a maiden who is about to be raped. Not knowing which to save, he prays that Christ defend Lionel, then goes to help the lady. He meets a seeming priest who falsely interprets Bors' visions and guides him to a lady who slays herself because he will not lie with her. In that instant the lady, her attendants, her tower, and the false priest all vanish in howling smoke.

A true priest explains that Lionel, a knight who has needlessly killed, is the rotten tree of Bors' vision, while the rapist and threatened maiden are the lilies: in choosing them Bors has chosen correctly, for they were still sinless, unlike Lionel. The battle he fought as a lady's champion was a battle for the New Law, Holy Church (represented also by the humble black bird of his dream), against the Old Law and the Devil, represented by the outwardly white bird.

Bors leaves and soon meets Lionel, free now and armed. Lionel tries to kill him for his choice of the lady rather than himself, and when a holy man throws himself over Sir Bors to save him, Lionel kills the holy man. He then kills another knight who tries to save Bors, and Bors prepares to kill Lionel. A fiery cloud parts them and Bors is ordered to flee to where Percival awaits him.

7. Sir Galahad

After many adventures, Galahad comes to a castle where there is a great battle going on. He helps the weaker party, giving Gawain the worst wound of his life and thus fulfilling the curse of which Launcelot spoke when he saw the sword in the floating stone.

Galahad then goes to a castle and there a lady asks him to follow her to the "highest adventure that ever any knight saw." She takes him to the ship of Percival and Bors. They travel until they come to another ship. When they board it they find it splendidly adorned but empty. It is the ship of faith, and none but steadfast believers are safe there. The lady who has led the knights here is Percival's sister; she warns Galahad not to enter unless he is sinless. He enters, saying he will be glad to die if he is found tainted, and finds a splendid sword and crown. Neither Bors nor Percival is proved fit to grip the sword, but Galahad achieves it. Percival's holy sister tells the three knights the history of the sword and scabbard and they leave with it.

They come to a castle where they miraculously slay many enemies of God. A holy man tells them the story of the castle, directs them to the Wasteland, and dies. On the way the three knights have further visions, then come with their guide to the castle of the sick lady and are forcefully urged to yield to the custom of the castle—a silver dish of blood from the maiden's arm. The three knights fight, but when Percival's sister understands the custom she yields to it. Knowing she is dying, she asks to be placed on a ship, saying she will be found under a tower at the holy city of Sarras, where all of them will be buried. A voice then tells the three knights they are to be parted until they arrive at the hall of Pellam, the Maimed King. Sir Bors rides away to rescue a wounded knight; Percival and Galahad ride on.

8. The Castle of Corbenic

Guided by a voice, Launcelot enters the ship of Percival's dead sister. After a month he meets Sir Galahad at a landing and takes him aboard. They sail on together, encountering many adventures. Half a year passes; then a white knight brings Galahad a horse and calls him out of the ship and Launcelot's company. A voice tells them they are parting until Judgment Day. Launcelot finds his way to Castle Corbenic, where the Grail is, and gets a glimpse of the Grail but is struck down and thus miraculously prevented from drawing near. He lies in a coma for twenty-four days, then leaves the castle and turns back to Camelot.

9. The Miracle of Galahad

Galahad comes to King Mordrayns (or Evelake), who has waited for him for four hundred years. Mordrayns embraces him and dies. Galahad rides on and comes to the lake of fire, a symbol of lechery (traditionally an emblem of hell itself). He puts his hand in the water and it cools. Then in the country of Gore, Galahad visits a burning tomb. The fire ceases and the body that has lain burning in the tomb for three hundred and fifty-four years, in punishment for a sin against Joseph of Aramathy, is reburied at Galahad's command.

At last he finds Percival and Bors, and they all ride to Corbenic, the Castle of the Maimed King, Pellam. There they see marvels and Galahad heals Pellam. Now Galahad, Bors, and Percival are guided to their ship, where they find the Grail. Galahad prays and is granted the right to choose his time of death. At last they arrive at Sarras, where Percival's dead sister awaits them, as predicted. Galahad heals a cripple.

Immediately afterward, the three knights are thrown into prison by a Saracen; but prison is no discomfort—the Grail comes to them and spreads feasts. After a time the Saracen king falls sick, calls them out of prison to ask their forgiveness, and dies. The city, guided by a voice out of heaven, makes Galahad king. At the year's end, Galahad sees a vision of Christ among his angels and asks to be raised to Him. He dies and his two friends see his soul borne to heaven. Percival becomes a religious hermit; Bors eventually returns to Arthur's sadly diminished court.

Commentary

In the Grail section the underlying weakness and futility of Arthur's court, which up to now Malory has only suggested by ironic juxtapositions, is laid out openly: Merlin's Round Table is a figure for the world, in medieval Christian doctrine the source of three dangerous temptations—"lust of the flesh, lust of the eyes, and pride of life" (see 1 John 2:16), that is, sinful concupiscence, covetousness, and overweening pride. Whatever the original function of the *lady* in Arthur's world, she has become in the end not the genteel embodiment of social judgment but the object of sexual lust; whatever the original function of knightly accouterments, titles, and lands, they have degenerated into things sinfully coveted; and chivalric heroism has in the same way degenerated into sinful pride.

Along with these central Christian tenets, a number of less-central Christian virtues are introduced in the Grail section to comment on what is wrong with Arthur's world. It is a world which cannot distinguish clearly between appearance and reality, or, in Christian language, outer appearance and inner meaning—surface and allegory. It is a world which thrives on legalized murder, forgetting the law "Thou shalt not kill"; a world in which fathers war with sons (one of the *leitmotivs* in Isaiah). Or to put all this another way, it is the eye-for-an-eye world of the Old Law, which must be overthrown by the New Law of charity.

The lucidity and conviction of Malory's Grail section are no doubt in large measure reflections of the personal religious feeling of the writer; but they are also effects of brilliant technique. Nearly everything Malory has done before, nearly every symbol and convention he has established earlier, he repeats here in a new context—the context of spiritual quest. For instance the convention of the borrowed shield, established in "Launcelot du Lake" and developed in every conceivable way in later tales, gets its final twist in the Galahad story: Galahad jousts with no shield at all, protected by grace (like Launcelot among the lions, later in the Grail section), then gets his red-cross shield from an agent of God. The convention of the guiding damsel, with its overtones of love between the guided and the guide, reappears here in idealized form: Percival and his friends are guided by Percival's sister, whose saintly love has nothing to do with *eros*.

Experiences of Arthur's worldly court which helped to define his worldly code have echoes here and define a higher

68

code. As Gawain mercilessly struck off the head of a lady who threw herself over her knight, Lionel strikes off the head of a holy man who throws himself over a knight to prevent a murder. As Pellanor sinned against the worldly code through the haste of his quest, Gawain sins against the higher code by haste: he cannot stop for counsel from a holy man. Parallels of this sort, though not necessarily schematic, are numerous.

The fundamental idea behind the Grail section is spelled out in the passage entitled "The Miracles." For all their loyalty to King Arthur, Launcelot and all worldly knights are guilty, finally, of "treason": the true king is Christ, and the true knightly code is not Arthur's but God's—chastity (at best, virginity), charity and abstinence (as opposed to covetousness), and humility (as opposed to knightly pride).

VII. SIR LAUNCELOT AND QUEEN GUINEVERE*

1. The Poisoned Apple

After the Grail Quest, Sir Launcelot soon falls to his old adulterous love again, despite his good intentions. But the queen, irrationally jealous because of his long absence from her on the Grail Quest, banishes him. To show that she is not grieved by his departure, she has a feast. There a knight is poisoned. Guinevere is falsely accused of the murder and condemned to burn: no man there will take her part. She goes to Launcelot's friend Bors, who agrees to be her champion provided no better knight can be found; he then tells Launcelot, who comes to fight for her. He overcomes Sir Mador and frees the queen. Nineve, the Lady of the Lake, reveals the true murderer, Sir Pinel, who intended the apple for Gawain as vengeance for the murder of Lamerok.

2. The Fair Maid of Astalot

Arthur orders a joust and asks Guinevere to go with him. She says she is sick, and Launcelot, not yet healed from Mador's

*For commentary on the whole Launcelot and Guinevere section, see p. 71.

strokes, also stays behind. Guinevere points out to Launcelot what gossips will say, and he decides to go after all, but not on the king's side. He lodges with the father of the Fair Maid of Astalot, who falls in love with him and begs him to wear her sleeve as a token of love. Launcelot decides to do so, because he has never worn a lady's token and this will make his disguise complete.

Launcelot and Sir Lavine, brother to the Lady of Astalot, fight brilliantly in the tournament, and only King Arthur knows who Launcelot is. Launcelot wins the field but is wounded almost mortally. He flees and Lavine helps him to a hermit. Sir Gawain, pursuing the disguised knight he has wounded, discovers that he is Launcelot and reports the sad news to the queen. When Guinevere hears that Launcelot wore the token of another lady she is furious.

Bors comes to Astalot, tells Launcelot of the queen's wrath and also of a forthcoming tournament where Launcelot can perhaps win back her love; then stays with him while his wounds heal. Earlier than he should, Launcelot gets out of bed, arms himself, and rides to see if he is strong enough to joust. His wounds reopen and he nearly bleeds to death. He is again put to bed, and Bors goes on without him. For all Bors can say, the queen remains furious. Gawain, Bors, and Gareth do better than any other knights — Gareth best of all — but Gareth rides away without stopping for his prize and so forfeits it.

Launcelot meanwhile leaves Astalot, and the lady dies of grief. She asks that her body be placed in a barge and that a letter telling her story be placed in her dead hand. The barge arrives at Camelot, and Guinevere understands the injustice she has done to her lover.

3. The Great Tournament

Arthur proclaims a tournament. Guinevere asks Launcelot to ride there wearing her token and requires him to make the token known to all of his own house so that they will not fight him. He agrees, then retires to rest and wait for the appointed day. As he lies beside a well a lady huntress accidentally shoots him with an arrow and thus weakens him; but Launcelot fights anyway, with Lavine at his side. Gareth joins him against Arthur's knights, and the three are the heroes of the day.

4. The Knight of the Cart

The queen decides to go on a May Day ride with her ten knights—unarmed except for swords—along with their ladies and their servants. Since Launcelot is not going to be among them, Sir Melliagaunce, who has long lusted after the queen, decides to attack her party and ravish her. Guinevere's knights fight but are overmatched, and to save their lives the queen agrees to go with Melliagaunce. She gets a message off to Launcelot, and he comes after her. When Melliagaunce's archers kill his horse he seizes a woodcart and comes in that. Melliagaunce pleads through the queen for mercy and, though still furious at the murder of his stallion, Launcelot pardons Melliagaunce.

That night Launcelot goes to the queen's room, tears an iron grill from her window, cutting his hand, and at her request lies with her. Melliagaunce sees the blood on the bed in the morning and accuses her of faithlessness to Arthur. To save Guinevere from execution at the stake, Launcelot says he will be her champion and sets a day for trial by battle.

Melliagaunce treacherously drops Launcelot through a trapdoor into a dungeon, but Launcelot escapes through the love of his lady jailor. When he has beaten Melliagaunce he offers to end the fight with one hand lashed to his body and his left side exposed, for he would rather fight thus than grant Melliagaunce mercy. Melliagaunce stupidly accepts the offer and dies.

5. The Healing of Sir Urry

Sir Urry, grieved by seven wounds that will never heal until the wounds have been treated by the best knight in the world, comes to Arthur's court at Pentecost. Arthur and all his court try to help him, but only Launcelot is effective, not through his own virtue but through his humble appeal to the Trinity. Urry follows Launcelot from that day forward, along with Sir Lavine. But on the night of the miraculous healing, Gawain's wicked brothers, jealous of Launcelot's success, lie in wait for him in the queen's bedroom, hoping to catch him with her.

Commentary

If *Le Morte Darthur* ended with the Grail section, its message would be one of ascetic Christianity: renounce the world. But it does not. Galahad's way may be the best, but it is not of this world. Launcelot is the best possible *worldly* man. Malory, in other words, rejects all-or-nothing Christianity, or at any rate allows degrees of virtue. So important is this point, in fact, that he repeatedly drops his usual narrative manner to introduce in this section direct address to the reader. This, for instance:

> Therefore, lyke as May moneth flowryth and floryshyth in every mannes gardyne, so in lyke wyse lat every man of worshyp florysh hys herte in thys worlde: firste unto God, and nexte unto the joy of them that he promysed hys feythe unto; for there was never worshypfull man nor worshypfull woman but they loved one bettir than another; and worshyp in armys may never by foyled. But firste reserve the honoure to God, and secundely thy quarell muste com of thy lady. And such love I calle vertuouse love.
> (from the opening of "The Knight of the Cart")

Launcelot's first loyalty is to Guinevere. That is his sin, and he admits it. But his sin is mitigated by the fact, first, that he has learned humility—whatever good he can do (for instance, the healing of Urry) he does by God's might, not his own—and by the fact that, second, it is not unnatural in a "worshypfull" man to love one woman "bettir than another."

Reserving "the honoure to God" and fighting not for his own sake but for his lady, Launcelot is the ideal embodiment of "vertuouse love." In "The Poisoned Apple" he fights for his lady's life, despite her cruel treatment of him. (It should be observed, however, that Malory's moving presentation of Guinevere's irrational jealousy makes her treatment of Launcelot not

72

so much "cruel" as poignantly and infuriatingly feminine, so that Launcelot's return to defend her comes as no surprise.) In "The Fair Maid of Astalot" he fights because to stay away might be to endanger her reputation. In "The Great Tournament" he fights because she asks him to — and fights despite a wound which makes it all but impossible for him to ride.

"The Knight of the Cart" introduces new complications: here Launcelot does *not* fight, though he wants to with all his heart, and the reason is that Guinevere forbids it. (Launcelot's huge and beautiful horse has been stupidly murdered by Melliagaunce's archers. Torn apart by arrows fired by cowards who will not stand and fight, the horse trails its master until it drops. When Guinevere sees Launcelot approaching on his cart, Malory says, "she was ware where cam hys horse after the charyotte, and ever he trode hys guttis and hys paunche undir hys feete." Malory could hardly have provided more shockingly dramatic justification for the rage Launcelot stifles at his queen's request.)

At the end of "The Great Tournament," on the other hand, Launcelot kills Melliagaunce because, looking to the queen for a signal, he sees that "anone the quene wagged hir hede uppon sir Launcelot, as ho seyth 'sle hym.'" He offers to lash one hand behind his back and fight with his left side exposed because he cannot honorably slay a beaten knight otherwise. "The Healing of Sir Urry," a secular parallel to Galahad's healing of the Maimed King, is Malory's dramatic demonstration that within his sphere Launcelot is virtuous.

But the fact remains, Launcelot's absolute faithfulness to Guinevere forces him into a loyalty conflict. He now jousts consistently on the side opposed to King Arthur. Worshipfully loving "one bettir than another," Launcelot has had to choose between queen and king.

VIII. THE DEATH OF KING ARTHUR*

1. Slander and Strife

Gawain's brothers Aggravain and Mordred, hating the queen and Launcelot, speak of their adulterous love before numerous knights. Gawain, Gareth, and others ask them to say no more and expect no support from them. Aggravain and Mordred nevertheless inform Arthur, who in fact has known for a long time and has ignored the matter for love of them both. He grudgingly consents to Aggravain's plan to trap them. The jealous brothers spring their trap; Launcelot kills Aggravain with twelve of his knights and wounds Mordred, who flees.

Arthur judges Guinevere to be burned, as law requires. Gawain pleads against it and refuses to have any part in it; his brothers Gareth and Gaheris beg to be excused as executioners or guards. All Launcelot's house urges him to rescue the queen, as he himself desires, and so when the queen is lashed to the stake Launcelot comes, kills all those standing around her — including Gareth and Gaheris, who are unarmed, and takes her with him to Joyous Gard, where Tristram kept Isode until King Mark murdered him.

2. The Vengeance of Sir Gawain

When Gawain hears of the death of his brothers he drops his love for Launcelot and swears he will be avenged. He persuades Arthur to lay siege to Joyous Gard. Arthur and Launcelot parley and Arthur is ready to drop the siege, but Gawain will not hear of it. The pope requires Arthur and Launcelot to make peace and orders Launcelot to return Guinevere to the king. Launcelot obeys; Gawain reaffirms his vow of vengeance; and Launcelot is banished — as was Tristram — and returns to his own country with all his forces.

3. The Siege of Benwick

At Gawain's insistence, Arthur attacks Launcelot's lands, leaving England and Guinevere in Mordred's safekeeping. Gawain fights nobly, but Launcelot will not come against him

*For commentary on the whole Death of Arthur section, see p. 76.

because of their former love. Finally, when Gawain calls Launcelot a traitor, shaming him before his people, Launcelot is forced to defend his honor. Launcelot beats Gawain but refuses to kill him.

Gawain is carried back to Arthur's tents and lies there three weeks to let his wounds heal. As soon as he can sit on a horse he challenges Launcelot again, and again Launcelot is forced to fight. He again hacks Gawain almost to death but stops at the last moment, leaving his former friend howling and whining in impotent rage. Then comes news of Mordred's treason.

4. The Day of Destiny

Mordred makes himself King of England and incestuously claims Guinevere as his wife. Guinevere escapes to the Tower of London. The Bishop of Canterbury reproaches Mordred for his usurpation and would-be incest, and when Mordred tries to kill him, he flees and becomes a hermit. Mordred wins many Englishmen to his side, then meets Arthur at Dover but is forced to retreat from him.

In this battle Gawain is mortally wounded. As he dies he admits to Arthur that if it were not for his insane pride in insisting on unjust revenge, Launcelot would be here now to save the kingdom; then he writes Launcelot, begging him to come help Arthur and also to pray at his tomb. Then, bleeding from the wound he got originally from Launcelot—with the fated sword of Balyn—Gawain dies.

Arthur meets Mordred again at the battle of Bareon Down and again puts him to flight. They meet next at Salisbury Plain, and there, with all who loved Launcelot fighting on Mordred's side, they prepare for what is to be their last battle. The night before the battle, Arthur dreams he is on the Wheel of Fortune, sitting on a throne and dressed in the richest gold that can be made:

And the kynge thought there was undir hym, farre from hym, an hydeous depe blak watir, and therein was all maner of

serpentis and wormes and wylde bestis fowle and orryble.
And suddeynly the kynge thought that the whyle turned up-
so-downe, and he felle amonge the serpentis, and every
beste toke hym by a lymme. And than the kynge cryed as he
lay in hys bed, "Helpe! helpe!"

After the prophetic dream he has another. Gawain and a number
of ladies come to him to warn him against fighting in the morning, for if Arthur fights he will die; if he waits for a month,
Launcelot will be here to help him. Then Gawain and the ladies
vanish.

Arthur asks a truce, and the two armies meet on the field to
set terms. An adder appears, a knight unthinkingly draws his
sword to kill it, and the two armies are at war. At the end of the
day, Mordred is the only man of his army left standing, and Arthur has only two knights, Sir Lucan and Sir Bedivere. Against
Sir Lucan's advice, Arthur fights Mordred and kills him, but he
gets his own death wound as he does it. Lucan and Bedivere
bear him to a chapel. Robbers overrun the battlefield stealing
the gear of dead knights, killing any that have life left in them.

Arthur is dying and cannot be moved to safety. And so he
sends Bedivere to throw Excalibur into the lake nearby, then
return and tell what he has seen. Bedivere hides the sword under
a tree, thinking it too precious to throw away, then returns and
says he has obeyed. "What did you see?" Arthur asks. Bedivere
says he saw only waves and winds. Arthur sends him twice more,
and the last time Bedivere does as he has been commanded. A
hand catches the sword and brandishes it three times.

Then at Arthur's command Bedivere carries the king to the
waterside, where a barge awaits him and some ladies in black
hoods. Bedivere puts Arthur in the barge and he is borne away
to Avilon, perhaps to heal his wounds, perhaps to die. Bedivere
wanders through a forest until he comes to where a hermit is
kneeling over a fresh grave. It is the grave of a man brought to
him at midnight by ladies in black. Whether or not the body is
really that of Arthur, no one knows. Some say Arthur still lives,
and some say not.

5. The Death of Sir Launcelot and Queen Guinevere

When Launcelot hears of the death of Arthur and Gawain, he comes to England in haste. He looks for the queen and finds her in a nunnery. For love of Guinevere as much as for remorse he takes on the habit of a priest. Guided by visions, he goes to Almesbury, where he finds Guinevere dead. He buries her beside King Arthur, then sickens and dies himself. He is buried at Joyous Gard. Constantine reigns after Arthur, but the scant remnants of the Round Table are dispersed. Bors, Ector, Blamour, and Bleoberis go to the Holy Land to fight the infidel. The rest simply wander off.

Commentary

The sword with which Arthur hacked civilization out of a wilderness was only a loan, whatever Arthur and the wizard-tempter who created him may have hoped. It is returned at last to the terrible Power which moves behind the jerking-puppet machinations of wizards and men, the Power to which Galahad and Launcelot pray. Triumphantly—and menacingly—the hand reaching out of the water brandishes the sword *three times.*

So, too, Guinevere's love for Launcelot was only a loan. She returns for the last time to sleep with her husband, and Launcelot dies, to be buried in the castle with the bitterly ironic name of "Joyous G[u]ard." The tragedy is finished.

REVIEW QUESTIONS

1. It has sometimes been argued that *Le Morte Darthur* was not originally intended as a unified legend but was merely a sequence of unrelated tales. Accordingly, Eugène Vinaver, in his great edition of Malory, used the title *The Works of Sir Thomas Malory.* (Professor Vinaver has since modified his position on the tales.) The present set of Notes on *Le Morte Darthur* assumes that the legend is unified, partly because that is the opinion which has won general acceptance; but the reader need not be limited by the point of view adopted in the Notes. What arguments can be advanced for

and against an interpretation of Malory's "works" as coherent legend?

2. Discuss Malory's narrative method, commenting on his apparent lack of interest in chronology of the sort usually found in the modern novel; his juxtaposition of plots and situations which serve to comment upon one another; his fondness for presenting crucial events offstage (e.g., the murders of Lot, Pellanor, Tristram, and Lamerok).

3. Trace Malory's development of Gawain's character. Is the characterization consistent? If it can be said that Gawain has certain consistent defects, can it also be said that he has consistent virtues?

4. Merlin sets up Arthur's kingdom partly through the agency of the Archbishop of Canterbury; the archbishop (sometimes called simply the bishop) also plays a part in the conclusion of the *Morte Darthur*. Is there any significance in this? Is there any significance in the fact that, like many of Arthur's knights, the archbishop at last becomes a hermit?

5. In the Grail section, both dreams and physical events are interpreted allegorically. Elsewhere Malory and his characters rest content, for the most part, with the outer appearance of things. To what extent, if any, do earlier and later adventures have allegorical as well as literary meaning?

6. Discuss Malory's use of symbolic settings in *Le Morte Darthur*—for instance, Tentagil, the Castle of Maidens, Joyous Gard, Benwick, the Castle of Corbenic, and so forth.

7. Discuss the interrelationship of the following motifs in Malory's work: courtly love, married love, the knightly vow of friendship, fealty, revenge, the ravishing of maidens, the murder of knights, Christian devotion, diabolism.

8. In what way does the feud between Lot's house and Pellanor's house contribute to the fall of the Round Table?

9. In *Le Morte Darthur* the medieval Christian ideal of renunciation of the world and the Renaissance concern with legitimate and illegitimate ambition stand in nervous equilibrium. Discuss this thesis as a means of accounting for Malory's ambivalent attitudes toward Launcelot, Gawain, Dynadin, and Tristram.

10. Point out specific instances of Malory's comic treatment of King Mark, Dynadin, and others, and comment on how the humor modifies Malory's theme.

11. What are the differences, for Malory, between ordinary people, witches or sorcerers, and devils?

12. Discuss *Le Morte Darthur* as a book for courtiers; as a book on kingship.

13. In "The Day of Destiny" Malory writes:

> Lo, ye all Englysshemen, se ye nat what a myschyff here was? For he that was the moste kynge and nobelyst knyght of the worlde, and moste loved the felyshup of noble knyghtes, and by hym they all were upholdyn, and yet myght nat thes Englyshemen holde them contente with hym. Lo thus was the olde custom and usayges of thys londe, and men say that we of thys londe have nat yet loste that custom.

In what specific ways does Malory's book "ended the ninth yere of the reygne of King Edward the Fourth" comment on the contemporaneous political situation?

14. Discuss the survival of pagan myth in *Le Morte Darthur*. To what extent do pagan myths seem to be more or less consciously manipulated here? (Consider Gawain's waxing and waning powers, the myth of the Wasteland and the king wounded in the thigh, etc.)

15. Either by close analysis of one tale in relation to its nearest sources or by examination of one tale and the studies of sources listed in the bibliography, show exactly what Malory did in composing any given tale, and point out the rele-

vance of Malory's additions or deletions to the theme of *Le Morte Darthur*.

SELECTED BIBLIOGRAPHY

Standard Edition

The Works of Sir Thomas Malory. Ed. EUGÈNE VINAVER in three volumes. Oxford at the Clarendon Press, 1947, reprinted with corrections, 1948. (For full bibliography to 1947, see VINAVER, pp. 1647 ff.)

Inexpensive Editions

SIR THOMAS MALORY. *King Arthur and His Knights*. Ed. EUGÈNE VINAVER (Original). Riverside Edition.

————. *The Morte D'Arthur*. Eds., C. R. SANDERS and C. W. WARD (Original). Appleton-Century-Crofts.

————. *Le Morte d'Arthur: King Arthur and the Knights of the Round Table: A New Rendition by Keith Baines* (Modernization). Mentor.

Books

J. A. W. BENNETT. *Essays on Malory*. Oxford at the Clarendon Press, 1963.

M. C. BRADBROOK. *Sir Thomas Malory* (Writers and Their Work, No. 95). London, 1958.

R. S. LOOMIS. *Arthurian Literature in the Middle Ages: A Collaborative History*. Oxford at the Clarendon Press, 1959.

R. M. LUMIANSKY, ed. *Malory's Originality: A Critical Study of the Morte Darthur*. Baltimore, 1964.

WILLIAM MATTHEWS. *The Ill-Framed Knight: A Skeptical Inquiry into the Identity of Sir Thomas Malory*. Berkeley and Los Angeles, 1967.

80

EUGÈNE VINAVER. *Malory*. Oxford, 1929.

VIDA D. SCUDDER. *Le Morte Darthur of Sir Thomas Malory: A Study of the Book and Its Sources*. London and New York, 1921.

Articles

BARBARA GRAY BARTHOLOMEW. "The Thematic Function of Malory's Gawain," *College English*, XXIV (1963), pp. 262-67.

R. T. DAVIES. "Malory's 'Vertuouse Love,'" *Studies in Philology*, LIII (1956), pp. 459-69.

R. M. LUMIANSKY. "Malory's 'Tale of Lancelot and Guinevere' as Suspense," *Medieval Studies*, XIX (1957), pp. 108-22.

CHARLES MOORMAN. "Courtly Love in Malory," *Journal of English Literary History*, XXVII (1960), pp. 163-76.

————. "Internal Chronology in Malory's *Morte Darthur*," *Journal of English and Germanic Philology*, LX (1961), pp. 240-49.

————. "Malory's Treatment of the Sankgreall," *Publications of the Modern Language Association*, LXXI (1956), pp. 496-509.

————. "The Relation of Books I and III of Malory's *Morte Darthur*," *Medieval Studies*, XXIII (1960), pp. 361-66.